Greek
phrasebook

Paul Hellander

P9-DSZ-945

Greek phrasebook
1st edition

Published by
  Lonely Planet Publications
  Head Office: PO Box 617, Hawthorn, Vic 3122, Australia
  Branches: 155 Filbert St, Suite 251, Oakland, CA94607, USA
       10 Barley Mow Passage, Chiswick, London W4 4PH, UK
       71 bis rue du Cardinal Lemoine, 75005 Paris, France

Printed by
  Colorcraft Ltd, Hong Kong

Cover Photograph
  Church, Santorini by Andrea Pistolesi (The Image Bank)

Published
  April 1995

About this Book
This book was written by Paul Hellander. It was edited by Sally Steward and designed by David Kemp. Illustrations by Maliza Kruh, Tamsin Wilson and others.
Valerie Tellini designed the cover. The author wishes to acknowledge all the travellers he has met over the years in Greece, his sons Byron and Marcus who keep him
going back there regularly. Special thanks to Stella Hellander, for her careful proof-
reading and suggestions, and to Aristotle University of Thessaloniki for an illustra-
tion from their book *Ta Nea Ellenika gia Xenous* (Thessaloniki, 1990).

National Library of Australia Cataloguing in Publication Data

Hellander, Paul D,
  Greek Phrasebook.

  1st ed.
  ISBN 0 86442 261 X.

  1. Greek language - Conversation and phrase books - English.
  I. Title. (Series : Lonely Planet language survival kit.)

489.383421

© Lonely Planet Publications Pty Ltd 1995

All rights reserved. No part of this publication may be reproduced, stored in a retrieval
system or transmitted in any form by any means, electronic, mechanical, photocopy-
ing, recording or otherwise, except brief extracts for the purpose of review, without the
written permission of the publisher and copyright owner.

Contents

Introduction

Modern Greek is the language of about 9.5 million people in Greece and the Greek islands and about half a million in Cyprus. It is also spoken in isolated villages in Turkey and southern Italy, and wherever Greeks have migrated, notably Australia and North America where there are around five million speakers. It has been argued that Melbourne in Australia is the third largest Greek-speaking city in the world: the Greeks of Chicago also claim the title!

Greek has had a huge influence on the history and culture of Europe; the international languages of science and philosophy, in particular, have borrowed heavily from it. The Greek language, which can be traced back as far as 1500 BC, is a member of the Indo-European family of languages; a huge language group which includes Germanic, Romance and Slavic languages. From the 4th century BC, after a thousand years of Greek dialects, a standard variety of Greek known as Koine became the common language. Modern Greek derives directly from Koine. In more recent times Greek met with the unfortunate fate of diglossy – the existence of two forms of the language. There was a formal (artificial) form called Katharevusa, or purist Greek, and a secular form spoken by everyone, called Demotic, or popular Greek. Katharevusa is now no longer used, and will only occasionally be met in some older official documents.

Greek, unlike Latin, never spawned a generation of new languages, so no language can be used as a convenient springboard to learn Greek in the way that, say, Italian can be used to learn Portuguese or Romanian. It is this fact, coupled with a theoretically difficult alphabet, that has given rise to such expressions as 'It's all Greek to me…'. Nonetheless, Greek is no more difficult

INTRODUCTION

than most Indo-European languages. Its pronunciation rules are more logical than those of English, and the grammar is no harder than German.

To anyone new to the language, Greek can sound fast, staccato and quite incomprehensible. In fact, Greeks speak no faster than anyone else: the impression may be created because they tend to be animated in their speech. Once the ear becomes attuned to separating individual words – as in the case of learning any language – it becomes quite accessible.

One major obstacle is the alphabet. English uses the Roman alphabet which is directly derived from the Greek (which, in turn, is derived from the Semitic alphabet, brought to Greece by the Phoenicians). So the difference btween the English and Greek alphabets is not that big. There are 24 letters of which approximately a third look similar to, or the same as, the Roman alphabet equivalents and have similar sounds. Another third look like Roman alphabet letters but have differing sounds. Only about eight letters are essentially new learning. So there is no real excuse not to learn the Greek alphabet when visiting Greece or Cyprus.

Accent differs from region to region and some accents may be more difficult to understand than others, but overall there is a general homogeneity in the everyday language. The electronic media, as elsewhere, has played its part in levelling language differences. As a visitor to Greece, your efforts to speak Greek will be richly rewarded, particularly as a lot of tourists don't make the effort.

This phrasebook aims to open up communication and help you make friends, as well as helping you get out of any sticky situations. While the dialogue will be for the most part one-way – to make yourself understood – as you learn more Greek by listening to responses, your comprehension level will increase and so will your satisfaction and enjoyment of your stay in Greece and Cyprus. Communication and mutual understanding are the keys to peace and harmony. Your efforts at speaking Greek will not only reward you personally, but will do their bit in breaking down cultural and linguistic barriers that for too long have been the cause of war and strife.

Help!

There are always essential words you need to know in a language. To begin with, learn *kalimera* (Good morning) and *kalispera* (Good evening) to get you through the day. *Efharisto* (thank you) is easy, as is *parakalo* (please). For other easy essentials, see page 43. If you don't understand or are stuck for words, try page 56. How much? is *poso?*

Don't be put off by the fact that you may not have time to learn any verbs. All essential verbs are in the Vocabulary chapter – just use them in their dictionary form and people will understand. If you're talking of a future action, throw in the word *tha* before the verb form. If it's already happened, learn a key word such as *ithi* (already) or *hthez* (yesterday).

Abbreviations Used in This Book

adj – adjective
f – feminine
inf – informal
m – masculine
n – neuter
pl – plural
sg – singular

Pronunciation

Greek is not difficult to pronounce, despite the formidable-looking initial barrier of the alphabet. Bear in mind that there are essentially only five 'pure' vowel sounds in Greek, though there may be some variation in the length, and that there are only one or two consonant sounds that take a bit of getting used to. You should find the pronunciation guides throughout the book useful not only for attempting a word or phrase but also for reminding yourself, when you hear a word or phrase, of how it sounded.

The Alphabet

The following alphabet shows the Greek letters in both capitals and lower case letters, the letter in English that it corresponds to and which we have used throughout the book as a guide, and an explanation of the sound. These explanations can only ever be approximate.

A α	**a**	as in standard British 'b**u**t'
B β	**v**	as in '**v**an'
Γ γ	**gh, y**	somewhere between a hard 'g' as in 'got' and 'y'(before'a' and 'o' ou') then like 'y' (before'e', 'i'). Takes a bit of practice.
Δ δ	**dh**	as in '**th**en'
E ε	**e**	as in 'th**e**n'
Z ζ	**z**	as in '**z**oo'
H η	**i**	as in 'p**i**n'
Θ θ	**th**	as in '**th**ick'
I ι	**i**	as in 'p**i**n'
K κ	**k**	as in '**k**ing'

11

Λ λ	l	as in 'lamp'
M μ	m	as in 'mad'
N ν	n	as in 'not'
Ξ ξ	x	as in 'axe'
O o	o	as in the British 'hot'
Π π	p	as in 'pin'
P ϱ	r	as in 'run', but slightly trilled
Σ σ	s	as in 'sand'
ς	z	as in 'plays', found only at the end of a word
T τ	t	as in 'ten'
Y υ	i	as the 'y' in 'many'
Φ φ	f	as in 'food'
X χ	h, ch	'ch' as in Scottish 'loch', but more aspirated (before a', 'o' and 'ou'). Before 'i' and 'e' it is pronounced like the 'h' in 'hee-hee'). Another tricky one!
Ψ ψ	ps	as in 'lapse'
Ω ω	o	as in the British 'hot'

Vowels

There are only five basic vowel sounds. These five sounds correspond to 'a' 'e' 'i' 'o' and 'u' as pronounced in their 'pure' form (i.e. as in 'but', 'bet', 'beet', 'bot', 'boot'). Try to imagine your mouth as a triangle, looking from the side: 'a' is formed low down towards the front; 'e' is pronounced higher up and a little further back; 'i' is pronounced at the apex of the triangle, in the middle of the palate; 'o' is pronounced further back and lower down and 'u' is pronounced at the third corner of the triangle, with the lips pursed.

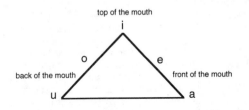

top of the mouth

back of the mouth

front of the mouth

Diphthongs

Greek has some interesting diphthong combinations (that is, combinations of two letters), but the basic pronunciation pattern of vowel sounds never changes. Consider the following Greek diphthongs and their pronunciations.

αι	**e**	as in 'th**e**n'
οι	**i**	as in 'p**i**n'
ει	**i**	as in 'p**i**n'
υι	**i**	as in 'p**i**n'

These last three sounds, plus 'ι', 'η' and 'υ', all sound the same.

ου	**u**	as in 'm**oo**d'
αυ	**av, af**	as in '**av**erage' or '**af**ter'
ευ	**ev, ef**	as in 's**ev**en' or 'l**ef**t'

In both the preceding cases, the pronunciation depends on whether the following sound is 'voiced' (i.e. pronounced with a sound from the larynx, like 'b' or 'd'), or unvoiced, like 'p' or 't'. In most cases, if you pronounce the words naturally, you will get the correct sound.

Consonants

It is generally agreed that correct vowel pronunciation makes or breaks a good 'accent' when speaking a language other than your own. Well, if you can get your tongue around the consonants as well, you are well on your way to sounding fluent at least.

There are two main areas of difficulty with Greek: these are the letters 'γ' and 'χ'. The difficulty is not in the pronunciation, but in the fact that there are no real equivalents in standard English. The best strategy, once you arrive in Greece or Cyprus, is to listen out for these sounds and practise them a few times.

The letter 'γ', when occurring before the 'a', 'i' and 'ou', sounds is like an English 'g' with the back of the throat open. Try it and see what happens when you don't close the back of the throat with your tongue. Before 'e' and 'i' it naturally sounds like the 'y' in 'yes'.

Similarly, the Greek letter 'χ' when pronounced before 'a', 'o' and 'ou' is pronounced like the 'ch' in the Scottish word 'loch'. With 'e' and 'i' the passage to the throat becomes naturally narrowed and the 'ch' sound becomes more like a hissing sound.

Some other consonant clusters that you need to be aware of are as follows:

μπ	**b, mb**	as in '**b**ed' at the beginning of a word; 'mb' in the middle of a word
ντ	**d, nd**	as in '**d**og' at the beginning of a word; 'nd' in the middle of a word
γκ	**g**	as in '**g**o'
γγ	**ng**	as in 'si**ng**er'
γχ	**nch**	as in 'bro**nchi**al'
τσ	**ts**	as in 'ha**ts**'
τζ	**dz**	as in 'a**dze**'

Double consonant clusters such as σσ, λλ, μμ, or ϱϱ are normally pronounced the same as the one consonant. Some regional differences will accentuate the pronunciation of the cluster.

Stress

The only really comforting rule here is that Greek is only stressed on one of the final three vowels. Some comfort when you consider the length of some Greek words. Stress, overall, tends to be even and perhaps staccato-sounding to the newcomer's ears. Questions are often formulated simply by raising the voice at the end of a sentence. Consider the question:

Do you sell newspapers?
poulate efimeridhez?   Πουλάτε εφημερίδες;

(Note that the Greek question mark is an ';' sign.)

This could equally be a statement:

You sell newspapers.
poulate efimeridhez   Πουλάτε εφημερίδες.

The only difference is in the voice tone. In the question the voice rises towards the end of the sentence, whereas in the statement the voice simply falls.

You don't need to speak fast to be fluent. Some of the best speakers of Greek speak slowly. Speak precisely and clearly and follow the transliteration guidelines, whenever necessary.

Accenting Greek

Greek has only one accent these days – the acute (´) accent (you may still see a circumflex (^), which is equivalent to the acute). The acute is placed over vowels of more than one syllable to indicate stress, and it helps young Greeks and foreigners to pronounce the language with the correct stress. Common convention is to omit the accent from initial stressed capital letters eg. Αρτα (Arta – town in northern Greece famous for its bridge). Today's system is a far cry from the system of old with three different accents, two 'breathing' marks and the iota subscript. Those classicists among you may remember them with some fondness. Other than the acute accent there is also a diaeresis that is sometimes used over 'ι' and 'υ' as in 'ϊ' and 'ϋ'. The diaeresis is used to indicate the the two vowels next to each other should be pronounced separately. Such occurrence of these vowels can be found in Ιαμαϊκή (Jamaica), Σύδνεϋ (Sydney), Αδελαΐδα (Adelaide), Ταΰγετος (Taygetos).

Guide to the Transliteration

Any transliteration method for any language is bound to be problematic, especially if we take into account the differing speech patterns of all of you who are using this phrasebook. If the Greeks had a better way of representing their language in written form than the one they currently use, we would not be using a Greek alphabet now. The moral of the story is, try to learn the Greek alphabet – it's not as difficult as it may seem!

In the meantime, the transliteration method will make things easier for you. Stress is indicated by a **bold** letter, unless the word has only one syllable or double stress patterns.

Grammar

Greek grammar, despite popular misconceptions, is no more difficult than many grammars of languages in the Indo-European family group. The main drawback of Greek for newcomers is its generally unfamiliar vocabulary. As mentioned in the introduction, Greek does not have any closely related languages, so its vocabulary tends to be isolating for most people. However, Greek's rich contribution to the scientific language of English means that a few words may already be familiar to you.

Grammatical Terms

A number of terms are used in this chapter. Masculine, feminine and neuter refer to the classification of words (nouns) usually by their endings, rather than by any sense of physical gender, or sex, although nouns which are clearly feminine (e.g. woman, *yineka*, γυναίκα) are feminine, and likewise obviously masculine nouns

(e.g. man, *andras*, άντρας) are masculine. Neuter nouns refer to nouns without gender, such as inanimate objects. Neuter nouns can also be words like child, *pedhi*, παιδί, which is considered not to have reached sexual maturity. By and large the 'sex definition' ends here. Adjectives also have masculine, feminine and neuter endings dependent on the classification of the noun they refer to.

The term 'subject' refers to the noun which operates the verb. With a sentence such as 'the man sees', 'the man' is the subject, as he is 'seeing'. The 'object' is a noun that is affected by the verb. In this case, whatever it is that the man sees. The term 'possessive' is applied to a noun that relates directly to another noun.

Sentence Structure

Sentences, in general, follow the subject-verb-object pattern of English, but because we can tell who is doing what to whom in a Greek sentence by the endings of the words, we can just as easily swap the positions. Take the following example:

The man sees the woman.
   o andras vlepi ti yineka   Ο άντρας βλέπει τη γυναίκα.
                      (lit. the man sees the woman)

It follows a pattern familiar to English. But …

   ti yineka vlepi o andras   Τη γυναίκα βλέπει ο άντρας.
                      (lit. the woman is seen by the man)

… means exactly the same. Except that there is more 'punch' by leaving the subject of the verb (the man) until the end of the sentence. This convention is very common in Greek. The key to the unchanging sense of the sentence is in the word endings, so it's important to get a basic idea of these.

GRAMMAR

Articles

Definite Article

In English, the definite article is always one word: 'the'. In Greek there are 12 words corresponding to the definite article. This is not as bad as it seems once you've got used to the idea that words change to 'agree' grammatically with others in the sentence.

Singular

	Masculine		**Feminine**		**Neuter**	
Subject	*o*	ο	*i*	η	*to*	το
Object	*to(n)*	το(ν)	*ti(n)*	τη(ν)	*to*	το
Possessive	*tou*	του	*tis*	της	*tou*	του

Plural

	Masculine		**Feminine**		**Neuter**	
Subject	*i*	οι	*i*	οι	*ta*	τα
Object	*tous*	τους	*tis*	τις	*ta*	τα
Possessive	*ton*	των	*ton*	των	*ton*	των

So, in the example of 'the cat sees the dog', *i ghata vlepi to skilo*, η γάτα βλέπει το σκύλο, you can tell that the cat is the subject because of the *i, η*; the dog is the object because of the *to, το*. A good time to change the example: if we swap it around to 'the dog sees the cat', *o skilos vlepi ti ghata*, ο σκύλος βλέπει τη γάτα, you can see how the article changes.

Note that proper names in Greek eg. Kostas, Nikos, Eleni, etc always take the definite article.

Nikos ...	*o nikos ...*	ο Νίκος ...
Eleni is ...	*i Eleni ine ...*	η Ελένη είναι ...

Indefinite Article

The indefinite article, 'a' in English, works in a similar way to the definite (singular) article, having six different forms.

There is no plural, of course. For 'some' we use words like μερικοί *meriki* (m), μερικές *merikez* (f), or μερικά *merika* (n).

	Masculine		Feminine		Neuter	
Subject	*enas*	ένας	*mia*	μια	*ena*	ένα
Object	*ena(n)*	ένα(v)	*mia*	μια	*ena*	ένα
Possessive	*enos*	ενός	*myas*	μιας	*enos*	ενός

GRAMMAR

Nouns

Greek nouns are characterised by their gender. The most common way to identify the gender is to look at the article that accompanies it and then look at the ending. In general there are set 'rules', but there are always exceptions! The following table gives you some guidelines:

Masculine		Feminine		Neuter	
-os	-ος	-a	-α	-o	-ο
-as	-ας	-i	-η	-i(ma)	--(μ)α
-eas	-εας	-ou	-ου	-i	-ι
-is	-ης	-os	-ος	-en	-εν
-es	-ες			-an	-αν
-ous	-ους			-os	-ος
				-eas	-εας
				-imo	-ιμο
				-os	-ως

Generally speaking, words ending in -ς *(-s)* tend to be masculine; words ending in one of the three vowel combinations above tend to be feminine, and neuter has a mixture of both plus the letter -ν *(-n)*. Nouns ending in -ος, *(-os)* can be sometimes masculine, sometimes feminine and sometimes neuter. Nouns in -ας *(-as)* can be either masculine or neuter.

Just so that you have something to go on, here is a table showing how three typical nouns change their endings. Other nouns tend to work in a similar fashion. The noun endings here are shown separately from their stems, in order to make it easier for you to follow the changes.

Singular

	Masculine friend		**Feminine** daughter		**Neuter** wine	
Subject	*fil-os*	φίλ-ος	*kor-i*	κόρ-η	*kras-i*	κρασ-ί
Object	*fil-o*	φίλ-ο	*kor-i*	κόρ-η	*kras-i*	κρασ-ί
Possessive	*fil-ou*	φίλ-ου	*kor-is*	κόρ-ης	*kras-you*	κρασ-ιού

Plural

	Masculine friends		**Feminine** daughters		**Neuter** wines	
Subject	*fil-i*	φίλ-οι	*kor-ez*	κόρ-ες	*kras-ya*	κρασ-ιά
Object	*fil-ous*	φίλ-ους	*kor-ez*	κόρ-ες	*kras-ya*	κρασ-ιά
Possessive	*fil-on*	φίλ-ων	*kor-on*	κορ-ών	*kras-yon*	κρασ-ιών

GRAMMAR

It may all sound hard in theory, but there is quite a bit of duplication of endings and once you have the hang of the pattern of changes, you will soon be able to make the changes yourself for most other nouns.

the daughter is here (subject)
   i kori ine edho   η κόρη είναι εδώ
we see the daughter
   vlepoume tin kori   βλέπουμε την κόρη
the daughter's wedding
   o ghamos tis koris   ο γάμος της κόρης
                               (lit. the wedding of the daughter)

Pronouns
Personal Pronouns
Personal pronouns are seldom used, as the meaning of 'I', 'you', 'he, she, it' is built into the verbs themselves. One important thing to remember is that Greek has two forms of the word 'you': one to indicate one of you and the other to indicate several of you. The plural form is also used as a polite form of addressing someone. The singular form is only used with people you are really familiar with, to children or to animals. Stick with the plural 'you' and you won't offend anyone.

I	*egho*	εγώ	we	*emis*	εμείς
you	*esi*	εσύ	you (pl)	*esis*	εσείς
he	*aftos*	αυτός	they (m)	*afti*	αυτοί
she	*afti*	αυτή	they (f)	*aftez*	αυτές
it	*afto*	αυτό	they (n)	*afta*	αυτά

GRAMMAR

Subject Pronouns

me	*(e)mena*	(ε)μένα	us	*(e)mas*	(ε)μάς
you	*(e)sena*	(ε)σένα	you (pl)	*(e)sas*	(ε)σάς
him	*afto(n)*	αυτό(ν)	them (m)	*aftous*	αυτούς
her	*afti(n)*	αυτή(ν)	them (f)	*aftez*	αυτές
it	*afto*	αυτό	them (n)	*afta*	αυτά

The brackets around the Greek mean that sometimes the vowel is used and sometimes it is omitted.

For example, where some emphasis is required:

to me	*se mena*	σε μένα
I like it (emphatic)	*emena mou aresi*	εμένα μου αρέσει

Possessive Pronouns

Possessive pronouns – words to describe my, your, their, etc – are placed after the noun.

my	*mou*	μου	our	*mas*	μας
your	*sou*	σου	your	*sas*	σας
his	*tou*	του	their	*tous*	τους
her	*tis*	της			
its	*tou*	του			

The order in Greek is article-noun-possessive pronoun.

my friend	*o filos mou*	ο φίλος μου
your wife	*i yineka sas*	η γυναίκα σας
our house	*to spiti mas*	το σπίτι μας

GRAMMAR

Verbs

As with most European languages, Greek verbs offer an economy and subtlety not usually found in English. This is primarily because verbs indicate the subject of the action without 'subject markers' like the personal pronouns 'I', 'you', 'she', etc. Not that they don't exist in Greek; you can simply leave them out in most cases. The various tenses (indications of time in an action e.g. today, tomorrow, last year) are shown within the verb. Take the following example.

I used to walk.
  perpatousa
  Περπατούσα.

GRAMMAR

To Be

The verb 'to be' is irregular – that is, it doesn't conform to the pattern that most verbs follow when adding verb endings.

Present

I am	*ime*	είμαι
you are	*ise*	είσαι
he/she/it is	*ine*	είναι
we are	*imaste*	είμαστε
you are	*iste*	είστε
they are	*ine*	είναι

Future

I will be	*tha ime*	θα είμαι
you will be	*tha ise*	θα είσαι
he/she/it will be	*tha ine*	θα είναι
we will be	*tha imaste*	θα είμαστε
you will be	*tha iste*	θα είστε
they will be	*tha ine*	θα είναι

Past

I was	*imoun*	ήμουν
you were	*isoun*	ήσουν
he/she/it was	*itan*	ήταν
we were	*imastan*	ήμασταν
you were	*isastan*	ήσασταν
they were	*itan*	ήταν

To Have

This is a useful verb which has regular endings, so it serves as a good example for the way most verbs work. In the examples here we have separated the *stem* (the part of the verb that stays the same) from the *ending* in order to illustrate more clearly how the changes occur. Normally the verb would be written as one word.

I have	*eh-o*	έχ-ω
you have	*eh-is*	έχ-εις
he/she/it has	*eh-i*	έχ-ει
we have	*eh-oume*	έχ-ουμε
you have	*eh-ete*	έχ-ετε
they have	*eh-oun*	έχ-ουν

GRAMMAR

Passive & Active Verbs

Passive verbs are verbs that indicate a subject's action on itself. Active verbs are those that effect an action on someone, or something, else, i.e. subject onto object. The endings to passive verbs are quite unlike the active verbs. The verb 'wash', *pleno,* πλένω serves as a good example of a common verb which has both active and passive forms:

I wash myself. (passive)
   plen-ome   Πλέν-ομαι.
I wash my clothes. (active)
   *plen-o ta **rouha mou***   Πλέν-ω τα ρούχα μου.

Future

Future tense forms are always preceded by the word θα *(tha)*. The verb itself is constructed with various endings, and it is beyond the scope of this phrasebook to describe them in detail. However, if you use θα *(tha)* plus any verb in the present tense, it will be understood that you are talking of a future action.

GRAMMAR

Past

Unlike the future tense, there is no simple way to indicate that you are talking in the past tense. To help you get by, the past tenses of some key words are listed in the vocabulary section.

Imperative (Commands)

Imperatives are part of the verb system but only exist in two forms: informal and polite. Unless you are trying to rid yourself of some unwanted attention, (see page 202), you should normally use the polite form.

Commonly, an imperative consists of the verb stem plus an imperative ending:

Stop! (familiar 'you')		
stamata!		Σταμάτα!
Stop! (plural or polite 'you')		
stamatiste!		Σταματήστε!
Come here! (familiar 'you')		
ela dho!		Ελα δω!
Come here! (plural or polite 'you')		
elate dho!		Ελάτε δω!

Negatives

Making a verb 'negative' is easy. You simply put the word δεν *(dhen)* or δε *(dhe)* before the verb. If the verb begins with a vowel, use δεν *(dhen)*; if the verb begins with a consonant, use δε *(dhe)*.

I have …	*eho* …	Εχω …
I don't have …	*dhen eho* …	Δεν έχω …
I want …	*thelo* …	Θέλω …
I don't want …	*dhe thelo* …	Δε θέλω …

Modal Words

You use modal words when you want to modify a verb by saying,
for example, you can or want to, or should do something: e.g. 'I
want to buy a souvenir …'

Must

To say 'I must …' in Greek you have to go about it in a slightly
round about way. The word is πρέπει *(prepi)* – which roughly
translates as 'it is necessary that …'

I must talk to you.
   prepi na sou miliso   Πρέπει να σου μιλήσω.
                           (lit. it is necessary that I (to you) talk)

Can (To Be Able)

I can	*bor-o*	μπορ-ώ
you can	*bor-is*	μπορ-είς
he/she/it can	*bor-i*	μπορ-εί
we can	*bor-oume*	μπορ-ούμε
you can	*bor-ite*	μπορ-είτε
they can	*bor-oun*	μπορ-ούν

I can talk to you.
   boro na sou miliso   Μπορώ να σου μιλήσω.
                           (lit. I can (to you) talk)

GRAMMAR

Want

If you would like to say 'I'd like to .../I want to ...', you use a
mixture of future and imperfect forms of the verb.

I want	*thel-o*	θέλ-ω
you want	*thel-is*	θέλ-εις
he/she/it wants	*thel-i*	θέλ-ει
we want	*thel-oume*	θέλ-ουμε
you want	*thel-ete*	θέλ-ετε
they want	*thel-oun*	θέλ-ουν

I'd like to talk to you.

    tha ithela na sou miliso   Θα ήθελα να σου μιλήσω.
                                  (lit. I would like to (to you) talk).

Need

Another verb that you are likely to use is the verb 'need'. This
verb presents a new angle on the verb system, so it is worth making note of how it works. The verb 'to need' χρειάζομαι
(hriazome) has totally different endings to the few verbs we have
met, but there are quite a few verbs like it:

I need	*hriaz-ome*	χρειάζ-ομαι
you need	*hriaz-ese*	χρειάζ-εσαι
he/she/it needs	*hriaz-ete*	χρειάζ-εται
we need	*hriaz-omaste*	χρειάζ-όμαστε
you need	*hriaz-este*	χρειάζ-εστε
they need	*hriaz-onde*	χρειάζ-ονται

I need a taxi.

    hriazome ena taxi   Χρειάζομαι ένα ταξί.

Adjectives & Adverbs

Adjectives in Greek have similar word endings to the nouns they describe.

Here is the adjective 'good', καλός *(kalos)*. We have separated the adjective endings from the stem to make it easier to follow the changes.

Singular

	Masculine		**Feminine**		**Neuter**	
Subject	kal-*os*	καλ-ός	kal-*i*	καλ-ή	kal-*o*	καλ-ό
Object	kal-*o*	καλ-ό	kal-*i*	καλ-ή	kal-*o*	καλ-ό
Possessive	kal-*ou*	καλ-ού	kal-*is*	καλ-ής	kal-*ou*	καλ-ού

GRAMMAR

Plural

	Masculine		**Feminine**		**Neuter**	
Subject	kal-*i*	καλ-οί	kal-*ez*	καλ-ές	kal-*a*	καλ-ά
Object	kal-*ous*	καλ-ούς	kal-*ez*	καλ-ές	kal-*a*	καλ-ά
Possessive	kal-*on*	καλ-ών	kal-*on*	καλ-ών	kal-*on*	καλ-ών

So, how does this work in practice? Look at these examples.

| good man | *kalos andras* | καλός άντρας |
| good men | *kali andrez* | καλοί άντρες |

The good man speaks Greek. (subject)
*o kalos andras milaee
Ellinika*
Ο καλός άντρας μιλάει
Ελληνικά.

We see the good men. (object)

v*lepoume tous kalous andrez*	μλέπουμε τους καλούς άντρες.

The Greek of good men. (possessive)

ta *Ellinika ton kalon andron*	Τα Ελληνικά των καλών αντρών.

It works the same way for feminine and neuter nouns. In the vocabulary at the end of the book you'll see all adjectives listed with their masculine, feminine and neuter endings respectively.

Adverbs are generally easy to work out. They are the neuter plural forms of the adjectives, and normally end in -α *(-a)*. Some end in -ως *(-os)*.

Comparatives

Comparatives have their own forms, but in general still follow the basic pattern for endings. Take the adjective 'tall', *psil-os*, ψηλός. Here is how we say 'taller'.

tall (m)	*psil-os*	ψηλ-ός	taller	*psil-oteros*	ψηλ-ότερος
tall (f)	*psil-i*	ψηλ-ή	taller	*psil-oteri*	ψηλ-ότερη
tall (n)	*psil-o*	ψηλ-ό	taller	*psil-otero*	ψηλ-ότερο

The suffix -ότερος/η/ο, *(-oteros/i/o)*, takes the place of the normal ending. The plural endings follow the same pattern. The word bad', *kakos*, κακός 'is irregular, but the endings don't vary.

bad (m)	*kak-os*	κακ-ός	worse	*hir-oteros*	χειρ-ότερος
bad (f)	*kak-i*	κακ-ή	worse	*hir-oteri*	χειρ-ότερη
bad (n)	*kak-o*	κακ-ό	worse	*hir-otero*	χειρ-ότερο

Superlatives

Superlatives work exactly the same way as comparatives. The only difference is the addition of the definite article ο, η, το *(o, i, to)* before the comparative of the adjective.

the tallest (m)	*o psil-oteros*	ο ψηλ-ότερος
the tallest (f)	*i psil-oteri*	η ψηλ-ότερη
the tallest (n)	*to psil-otero*	το ψηλ-ότερο

the worst (m)	*o hir-oteros*	ο χειρ-ότερος
the worst (f)	*i hir-oteri*	η χειρ-ότερη
the worst (n)	*to hir-otero*	το χειρ-ότερο

GRAMMAR

Questions

Questions are generally formed by changing the voice tone, so the following statement becomes a question simply by the voice being raised towards the end, much the same as when, in English, we might ask 'You speak English?':

You speak English.
    milate ellinika   Μιλάτε ελληνικά.
Do you speak English?
    milate ellinika?   Μιλάτε ελληνικά;

what	*ti*	τι
who	*pios*	ποιος
where	*pou*	πού
how	*pos*	πώς
how much	*poso*	πόσο
how many	*posa*	πόσα
when	*pote*	πότε

Sorry, what did you say?		
signomi, ti ipate?	Συγγνώμη, τι είπατε;	
Who do I ask?		
pyon tha ritiso?	Ποιον θα ρωτήσω;	
Where is the bus station?		
pou ine o stathmos leoforion?	Πού είναι ο σταθμός λεωφορείων;	
How do I get to …?		
pos tha pao sto … ?	Πώς θα πάω στο …;	
How much is it?		
poso kani?	Πόσο κάνει;	
When will you know?		
pote tha xerete?	Πότε θα χέρετε;	

Prepositions

There is a wide variety of prepositions in Greek. They work much the same as their English counterparts, though most Greeks would agree that English prepositions are, by far, more difficult than Greek ones. One ubiquitous little preposition you will come across many times is σε *(se)* which can mean 'to', 'at', 'on', or 'in'. It commonly joins the definite article to make one word, dropping the ε:

on the …	*sto …*	στο…
to the …	*sti …*	στη…
in the …	*stous …*	στους…

Conjunctions

Conjunctions are linking words (such as 'and', 'but', 'then' etc) and in Greek work pretty much the same way as in English.

and	*ke*	χαι
because	*dhioti*	διότι
but	*alla*	αλλά
if	*ean*	εαν
or	*i*	ή
then	*tote*	τότε

Making Your Own Sentences

Remember the basic sentence formula subject-verb-object. Most importantly listen to the Greek you hear around you. Once you have started to get the hang of it, making your own sentences should be no more difficult than using the stock phrases in this book. Most of all don't be shy! Learning Greek is about listening to Greek and speaking Greek.

I need a ticket.
hriazome ena isitirio   Χρειάζομαι ένα εισιτήριο.
We need tickets.
hriazomaste isitiria   Χρειαζόμαστε εισιτήρια.
I need a room.
hriazome ena dhomatio   Χρειάζομαι ένα δωμάτιο.
I need a cheap room.
hriazome ena ftino   Χρειάζομαι ένα φτηνό
dhomatio   δωμάτιο.
Do you have a cheap room?
ehete ena ftino dhomatio? Εχετε ένα φτηνό δωμάτιο;

GRAMMAR

The bus is leaving.
to leoforio fevyi   Το λεωφορείο φεύγει.
The bus is going to …
to leoforio paee sto …   Το λεωφορείο πάει στο …
Where is the bus going to?
pou paee to leoforio?   Πού πάει το λεωφορείο;
My bags (luggage).
i aposkevez mou   Οι αποσκευές μου.
Our bags.
i aposkevez mas   Οι αποσκευές μας.
Can we leave our bags here?
boroume nafisoume tis   Μπορούμέ ν' αφήσουμε τις
aposkevez mas edho?   αποσκευές μας εδώ.
Can we?
boroume?   Μπορούμε;

GRAMMAR

Greetings & Civilities

Greetings

Like most people everywhere, Greeks have a set of stock phrases and expressions used when greeting one another, or a stranger. These are perhaps some of the most important words of Greek that you may need to know.

Greek men and women almost always shake hands when meeting up with one another and if they know one another well enough, will exchange kisses – men included! These basic expressions should be all you need to make an opening line.

Hello.
  ya sas/ya sou   Γεια σας/γεια σου. (inf)

Good morning.
  kalimera   Καλημέρα.

Good evening.
  kalispera   Καλησπέρα.

How are things?
  ti yinete?   Τι γίνεται;

What's new?
  ti nea?   Τι νέα;

How are you?
  ti kanete/ti kanis?   Τι κάνετε/Τι κάνεις (inf);

How are you going?
  pos ta pate?   Πώς τα πάτε;
  pos ta pas? (inf)   Πώς τα πας;

37

Goodbyes

When you are saying goodbye, it is common to say:

Pleased to have met you!
    harika poli!   Χάρηκα πολύ!
Goodbye!
    andio!   Αντίο!

Other expressions include:

Goodbye. (same as 'hello')
    ya sas/ya sou   Γεια σας/γεια σου. (inf)
So long!
    andio!   Αντίο!
See you!
    sto kalo!   Στο καλό!
Good night.
    kalinihta   Καληνύχτα.
Until we see each other
again!
    sto epanidhin!   Στο επανιδείν! (a bit formal)

Civilities

When meeting people, it is common courtesy to ask after members of their family.

How is ... ?	ti kani ...?	Τι κάνει ... ;
your father	o pateras sas	ο πατέρας σας
your mother	i mitera sas	η μητέρα σας
your wife	i yineka sas	η γυναίκα σας
your husband	o andras sas	ο άντρας σας
your mother-in-law	i pethera sas	η πεθερά σας
your father-in-law	o petheros sas	ο πεθερός σας

Forms of Address

The main point to watch out for here is the use of the polite and informal forms of address. In this book we have used the polite form throughout. You can usually start using the informal form when someone uses it with you, or when talking to children or animals.

When addressing someone directly you use the following terms:

Mr ...	kirie ...	Κύριε ...
Mrs ...	kiria ...	Κυρία ...
Miss ...	dhespinis ...	Δεσποινίς ...

The Greeks have not devised a term for Ms yet. Often, when addressing someone of status, or with a professional position, you will use that person's title.

Doctor ...	yatre ...	Ιατρέ ...
Professor ...	kirie kathiyita ...	Κύριε Καθηγητά ...
Director ...	kirie dhiefthinda ...	Κύριε Διευθυντά ...
Minister ...	kirie ipourghe ...	Κύριε Υπουργέ ...

It sounds a bit odd in English, but it is perfectly normal in Greek.

GREETINGS

Getting Someone's Attention

If you wish to attract someone's attention, you can use any of the titles listed earlier, or one of the following phrases.

Excuse me!	
me sinhorite!	Με συγχωρείτε!
I beg your pardon!	
sighnomi!	Συγγνώμη!
Just a moment!	
mya stighmi!	Μια στιγμή!
Please! (not a good transla-tion, but it works in Greek)	
parakalo!	Παρακαλώ!

You may notice that a man's name may change when people call out to him. There's no simple rule to this, but at least it only occurs amongst half the population – women's names never change.

Kostas, come here!	
Kosta, ela dho!	Κώστα, έλα δω!
Pavlos, I want to talk to you ...	
Pavle, thelo na sou miliso ...	Παύλε, θέλω να σου μιλήσω ...

Apologies

Should you make a mistake, you will normally be forgiven if you use one of the following expressions.

I am sorry.	
sighnomi	Συγγνώμη.

Please forgive me.
   me sinhorite   Με συγχωρείτε.

I am sorry if I offended you.
   sighnomi pou sas   Συγγνώμη που σας
   prosevala   προσέβαλα.

Body Language

Body language is a vital part of communication, so here are a few tips.

The main things to watch out for are the head gestures when saying 'no' and 'yes'. They are commonly the opposite of what you may be used to. A head turned from side to side – maybe just once – can mean 'yes' (ναι). A head thrown backwards once, or perhaps twice, means 'no' (όχι). Sometimes the 'no' gesture will be accompanied by a click of the tongue; sometime it is only just a roll of the eyes upwards. Watch out for these gestures, especially from kiosk vendors. Shrugged shoulders will often accompany a negative response to a question i.e. 'I don't know', *dhen xero*, δεν ξέρω.

Here are one or two common expressions you may pick up.

Sure! Too right!
   malista!   Μάλιστα!
You've got to be joking!
   astievese!   Αστειεύεσαι!
I don't think so… (more of
an exclamation)
   ba!   Μπα!

Common Expressions

Greek is rich in conversational 'fillers' and expletives. We'll leave
the more colourful forms of the latter for you to discover your-
selves. The following common ones will crop up everywhere you
go.

No worries!
   mi stenahoriese!   Μη στεναχωριέσαι!
OK!
   endaksi!   Εντάξει!
Who cares!
   dhe variese!   Δε βαριέσαι!
My God!
   the mou!   Θεέ μου!
Get away!
   aee hasou!   Αε χάσου!

Small Talk

Part of any Greek's interaction with another Greek will always consist of some small talk and exchange of pleasantries.

Top 10 Useful Phrases

The following are all-purpose expressions that you might need on the spur of the moment.

Yes.	*ne*	Ναι.
No.	*ohi*	Οχι.
Please.	*parakalo*	Παρακαλώ.
Thank you.	*efharisto*	Ευχαριστώ.
Hello!	*ya sas!*	Γεια σας
How are you?	*ti kanete?*	Τι κάνετε;
Pleased to meet you.	*hero poli*	Χαίρω πολύ.
Excuse me/sorry!	*me sinhorite/ sighnomi!*	Με συγχωρείτε/ συγγνώμη!
It doesn't matter/ that's all right.	*dhem birazi*	Δεν πειράζει.
Where is ...?	*pou ine ...?*	Πού είναι; ...

Don't be shy about talking to people in Greece. The Greeks are gregarious and will enjoy talking to you, especially if you can demonstrate some knowledge of Greek. Some questions may seem very forward to you, like whether you are married, what job do you do or how much you earn. People are very open about these subjects in Greece.

Meeting People

What is your name?
pos sas lene/pos legeste? Πώς σας λένε/πώς λέγεστε;
My name is …
me lene … Με λένε …

In rural areas in particular, Greeks don't ask one another what their name is, but 'whose are you?'. In other words, who is your father or, which family do you belong to.

tinos iste? Τίνος είστε;

Here, someone might reply …

I am Kostas' son/daughter.
ime tou Kosta o yios/ Είμαι του Κώστα ο γυιος/
i kori η κόρη.

If you'd like to introduce someone, try one of the following expressions:

I'd like to introduce you to …	*tha ithela na sas sistiso …*	Θα ήθελα να σας συστήσω …
my husband	*ston andra mou*	στον άντρα μου
my wife	*sti yineka mou*	στη γυναίκα μου
my boyfriend	*sto filo mou*	στο φίλο μου
my girlfriend	*sti fili mou*	στη φίλη μου
my son	*sto yio mou*	στο γυιο μου
my daughter	*stin gori mou*	στην κόρη μου
my father	*stom batera mou*	στον πατέρα μου
my mother	*sti mitera mou*	στη μητέρα μου

SMALL TALK

Special Occasions

Greeks have a whole range of everyday expressions from 'enjoy your meal' to 'congratulations (on buying some new item)'. They make wonderful ice-breakers and it might be a good idea if you learned a few of them by heart to use at the appropriate moment:

Cheers! (when raising your glass)
   stin iyia sas!   Στην υγεία σας!

Bon appétit!
   kali oreksi!   Καλή όρεξη!

Congratulations!
   sinharitiria!   Συγχαρητήρια!

Good luck!
   kali tihi!   Καλή τύχη!

All the best. (when someone is leaving)
   na pate sto kalo   Να πάτε στο καλό.

Happy birthday.
   hronia polla   Χρόνια πολλά.

Pay special attention to this last ubiquitous expression: it is used on several occasions other than birthdays. For instance, you say it for name days. A name day is the one day in the year where a saint is honoured and celebrated. If your name is the same as the saint, you celebrate that day as if it were your birthday (Greeks tend to celebrate these more than birthdays). You also say *hronia polla* at Christmas time, at New Year and on major public feasts. The expression literally means 'many years'.

If you are ever invited to a Greek home, a Greek wedding, or happen to be in Greece at Easter time – the most important time in the Greek religious calendar – you'll find it useful to learn some common expressions:

Welcome!	
kalos irthate!	Καλώς ήρθατε!
Nice to be here! (your response)	
kalos sas vrika!	Καλώς σας βρήκα!
Please take a seat.	
kathiste	Καθήστε.
What can I offer you?	
ti na sas keraso?	Τι να σας κεράσω;

You will invariably be offered a drink or a sweet snack, γλυκό (*ghliko*) and quite often it may be a preserved fruit in syrup, offered with a glass of water. It would not be polite to refuse such a gesture. You would normally say 'cheers' (lit. 'to your health') before first drinking your water, or other drink, though, oddly enough, not with coffee.

Christenings

At a christening, you would say to the parents:

Congratulations! (lit. may s/he live for many years)	
na sas zisi!	Να σας ζήσει!
All the best! (lit. may you enjoy your child)	
na to hereste!	Να το χαίρεστε!

SMALL TALK

Weddings

At a wedding, there are various formalised expressions of congratulation. At the line-up after the wedding, when everyone greets the bride and groom, the parents-in-law, the best man/woman and the bridesmaids, you say:

Congratulations! (to the couple
– lit. 'may you enjoy long life')
   na zisete!   Να ζήσετε!
Congratulations! (to the parents
– lit. 'may they live for many
years')
   na sas zisoun!   Να σας ζήσουν!
Congratulations! (to the best
man – lit. 'lucky')
   kalorizikos!   Καλορίζικος!
or, if it is a best woman …
   kaloriziki!   Καλορίζικη!
'Your turn next!' (to the bridesmaids, if they are single)
   ke sta dika sas!   Και στα δικά σας!

As you can see, Greeks take wedding greetings pretty seriously and these are only a few of the expressions.

Shopping

There are even expressions for when you buy something new. There are no real equivalents in English:

Congratulations! (for personal items
like clothing lit. 'with health')
   me ya!   Με γειά!
Congratulations! (for larger items
like a new car, lit. 'lucky')
   kaloriziko!   Καλορίζικο!

Easter

Easter is the main festive season in Greece and is taken very seriously, with much solemnity before Easter and much exuberance after Easter (the Resurrection). You will commonly hear the following expressions:

Happy Easter! (in the days
before Easter)
   kalo Pascha!   Καλό Πάσχα!
Happy Easter! (after the resurrection
at midnight before Easter Sunday,
lit. Christ has risen!)
   Christos anesti!   Χριστός ανέστη!

to which you reply ...

'He has risen, indeed'!
   alithos anesti!   Αληθώς ανέστη!

Churchgoers from the midnight Easter service will then wander off to their homes bearing candles with which they annoint the top of the door-frame at their house, forming the shape of a cross with the flame from the candle. They will then partake of the traditional midnight Easter dish called μαγειρίτσα *(mayiritsa)*, a kind of tasty (apparently!) entrail soup. On Easter Sunday itself, Greeks will often roast a whole lamb on a spit and families will gather to celebrate the feast with much eating and drinking. Greek Easter is an event not to be missed!

Nationalities

Where are you from?
apo pou iste?   Από πού είστε;

I am from …	*ime apo …*	Είμαι από …
Australia	*tin afstralia*	την Αυστραλία
America	*tin ameriki*	την Αμερική
Canada	*ton ganadha*	τον Καναδά
England	*tin anglia*	την Αγγλία
France	*ti Gallia*	τη Γαλλία
Germany	*ti yermania*	τη Γερμανία
Ireland	*tin irlandhia*	την Ιρλανδία
Japan	*ti yaponia*	τη Ιαπωνία
the Middle East	*ti mesi anatoli*	τη Μέση Ανατολή
New Zealand	*ti nea zilandhia*	τη Νέα Ζηλανδία
Scandinavia	*ti skandhinavia*	τη Σκανδιναβία
Scotland	*ti skotia*	τη Σκωτία
South Africa	*ti notia afriki*	τη Νότια Αφρική
Spain	*tin ispania*	την Ισπανία
Switzerland	*tin elvetia*	την Ελβετία
Wales	*ti wallia*	τη Γουαλλία

Age

How old are you?
poson hronon iste?   Πόσων χρονών είστε;
How old is your child?
poson hronon ine to pedhi   Πόσων χρονών είναι το παιδί
sas?   σας;
I am 24.
ime ikosi tesaron hronon   Είμαι είκοσι τεσσάρων χρονών.

Refer to page 165 for a full list of numbers.

Occupations

What is your occupation?
ti dhoulya kanete?   Τι δουλειά κάνετε;

I am a/an ...	*ime ...*	Είμαι ...
accountant	*loghistis* (m)	λογιστής
	loghistria (f)	λογίστρια
actor	*ithopiyos*	ηθοποιός
architect	*arhitektonas*	αρχιτέκτονας
artist (painter)	*zoghrafos*	ζωγράφος
businessman/	*epihirimatias*	επιχειρηματίας
businesswoman		
carpenter	*marangos*	μαραγγός
chef	*mayiras* (m)	μάγειρας
	mayirisa (f)	μαγείρισα
doctor	*yatros*	ιατρός
driver	*odhighos*	οδηγός
engineer	*mihanikos*	μηχανικός
farmer	*aghrotis* (m)	αγρότης
	aghrotisa (f)	αγρότισσα
fisherman/	*psaras*	ψαράς
fisherwoman		

homemaker	*nikokiris* (m)	νοικοκύρης
	nikokira (f)	νοικοκυρά
journalist	*dhimosioghrafos*	δημοσιογράφος
labourer	*erghatis* (m)	εργάτης
	erghatria (f)	εργάτρια
musician	*mousikos*	μουσικός
nurse	*nosokomos* (m)	νοσοκόμος
	nosokoma (f)	νοσοκόμα
office worker	*ipallilos ghrafiou*	υπάλληλος
		γραφείου
pastor/priest	*pappas*	παππάς
salesman	*politis*	πωλητής
saleswoman	*politria*	πωλήτρια
scientist	*epistimonas*	επιστήμονας
secretary	*ghramateas*	γραμματέας
soldier	*stratiotis*	στρατιώτης
student	*fititis* (m)	φοιτητής/
	fititria (f)	φοιτήτρια
teacher	*dhaskalos* (m)	δάσκαλος
	dhaskala (f)	δασκάλα
waiter	*servitoros* (m)	σερβιτόρος
	servitora (f)	σερβιτόρα
writer	*singhrafeas*	συγγραφέας

Some Useful Words

amateur	*erasitehnis*	ερασιτέχνης
job	*dhoulya*	δουλειά
retired	*sindaxiouhos*	συνταξιούχος
salary	*misthos*	μισθός
unemployed	*anerghos/i*	άνεργος/η

Religion

What is your religion?
ti thriskevma iste? Τι θρήσκευμα είστε;

I am a/an ...	*ime ...*	Είμαι …
Buddhist	*voudhistis*	Βουδιστής
Catholic	*katholikos/i*	καθολικός/ή
Christian	*hristianos/i*	χριστιανός/ή
Hindu	*indhouistis*	ινδουϊστής
Jewish	*evreos/evrea*	εβραίος/εβραία
Muslim	*mousoulmanos/a*	μουσουλμάνος/α
Protestant	*dhiamartiromenos/i*	διαμαρτυρόμενος/η

I am not religious.
dhen ime thriskeftikos/i Δεν είμαι θρησκευτικός/ή.

Some Useful Words

Bible	*evangelio*	Ευαγγέλιο
cathedral	*kathedhrikos naos*	καθεδρικός ναός
church	*ekklisia*	εκκλησία
god	*theos*	Θεός
monastery	*monastiri*	μοναστήρι
mosque	*tzami*	τζαμί
religion	*thriskevma*	θρήσκευμα
synagogue	*sinaghoghi*	συναγωγή
temple	*naos*	ναός

Family

See also Meeting People, page 44.

Are you married?
  iste pantremenos/
  pantremeni?
Είστε παντρεμένος/
παντρεμένη;

I am married.
  ime pandremenos/i
Είμαι παντρεμένος/η.

I am single.
  ime anipandros
Είμαι ανύπαντρος.

Do you have any children?
  ehete pedhya?
Εχετε παιδιά;

We have one (child).
  ehoume ena pedhi
Εχουμε ένα παιδί.

We don't have any
(children).
  dhen ehoume pedhya
Δεν έχουμε παιδιά.

Family Members

husband	*andra*	άντρα
wife	*yineka*	γυναίκα
boyfriend	*filo*	φίλο
girlfriend	*fili*	φίλη
son	*yio*	γυιο
daughter	*gori*	κόρη
father	*batera*	πατέρα
mother	*mitera*	μητέρα

SMALL TALK

Expressing Feelings

I am ...	*ime ...*	Είμαι ...
Are you ...?	*iste/ise ...?*	Είστε/είσαι ...
angry	*thimomenos/i*	θυμωμένος/η
happy	*haroumenos/i*	χαρούμενος/η
sad	*stenahoremenos/i*	στεναχωρεμένος/η
tired	*kourazmenos/i*	κουρασμένος/η
well	*kala*	καλά

Are you cold?
  krionete?   Κρυώνετε;
Are you hungry?
  pinate?   Πεινάτε;
This is great! (fun)
  ti kala!   Τι καλά!

Expressing Opinions

I think that ...
  nomizo pos ...   Νομίζω πως ...
I agree.
  simfono   Συμφωνώ.
I disagree.
  dhiafono   Διαφωνώ.
In my opinion ...
  kata ti ghnomi mou ...   Κατά τη γνώμη μου ...
It's (not) important.
  (dhen) axizi   (Δεν) αξίζει.

SMALL TALK

Language Difficulties

An expression well worth memorising:

Could you please write that
down?
    *sas parakalo, borite na
    mou to grapsete?*
        Σας παρακαλώ μπορείτε να
        μου το γράψετε;

You may find this useful whenever you need to know any precise
information – like a price, the time or an address. Other expressions that may help you are:

What does that mean?
    ti simeni afto?
        Τι σημαίνει αυτό;
Sorry, what did you say?
    signomi, ti ipate?
        Συγγνώμη, τι είπατε;
Could you please speak more
slowly?
    *borite na milisete pio
    argha?*
        Μπορείτε να μιλήσετε πιο
        αργά;
Just a minute! (eg while you
look something up)
    mya stighmi!
        Μια στιγμή!
I understand.
    katalaveno
        Καταλαβαίνω.
I see.
    katalava
        Κατάλαβα.
I don't understand.
    den katalaveno
        Δεν καταλαβαίνω.
Can you show me?
    borite na mou dhiksete?
        Μπορείτε να μου δείξετε;

I'll show you.
  tha sas dhikso   Θα σας δείξω.

If you are having real problems making yourself understood in Greek, you could always ask if someone speaks another language. Many Greeks have lived and worked abroad and there is usually someone who can speak another language:

Do you speak ...?   *milate ...*   Μιλάτε ... ;
Does anyone   *milaee kanees ...*   Μιλάει κανείς ... ;
speak ...?
  English   *anglika*   Αγγλικά
  French   *gallika*   Γαλλικά
  German   *yermanika*   Γερμανικά
  Italian   *italika*   Ιταλικά
  Swedish   *souidika*   Σουηδικά

Ice Breakers

friend   *filos/fili*   φίλος/φίλη
We're friends.   *imaste fili*   Είμαστε φίλοι.
We're relatives.   *imaste singenis*   Είμαστε συγγενείς.

I'm here on business.
  ime edho ya dhoulyez   Είμαι εδώ για δουλειές.
I'm on holiday.
  ime se dhiakopez   Είμαι σε διακοπές.
Nice weather, isn't it?
  poli oreos keros!   Πολύ ωραίος καιρός!
Are you waiting too?
  perimenete ki esis?   Περιμένετε κι εσείς;

SMALL TALK

Do you live near here?
   menete edho konda?   Μένετε εδώ κοντά;
What a cute baby.
   ti oreo moro   Τι ωραίο μωρό.

You're lucky. (fortunate)
   iste tiheros/i   Είστε τυχερός/ή.
We like it here.
   mas aresi edho   Μας αρέσει εδώ.
This is my address.
   afti ine i dhiefthinsi mou   Αυτή είναι η διεύθυνσή μου.
May I have your address?
   mou dhinete ti dhiefthinsi   Μου δίνετε τη διεύθυνσή
   sas?   σας;
Really!
   alithya!   Αλήθεια!
You're right.
   ehete dhikyo   Εχετε δίκιο.

You'll Hear

You'll hear street language all around you, and you won't always be able to work out what they are saying from looking in this book or in a dictionary.

Ελα ρε!	*ela re!*	Hey you!
Πω, πω!	*po po!*	My goodness!
Άϊντε, ντε!	*aeede de!*	Get away with you!
Σώπα καλέ!	*sopa kale!*	You've gotta be joking!

SMALL TALK

Finding Your Way

Many people speak English in Greece and are only too happy to help out. But this is not always the case in more out-of-the-way places. The phrases in this section should help you get out of all but the trickiest of situations.

How do I get to ...?	*pos tha pao sto ...?*	Πώς θα πάω στο …;
Where is ...?	*pou ine ...?*	Πού είναι …;
the bus station	*o stathmos leoforion*	ο σταθμός λεωφορείων
the train station	*o sidhirodhromikos stathmos*	ο σιδηροδρομικός σταθμός
the airport	*to aerodhromio*	το αεροδρόμιο
the subway station	*o stathmos tou Metro*	ο σταθμός του Μετρό
the taxi stand	*i stasi ton taxi*	η στάση των ταξί
the port	*to limani*	το λιμάνι
the ticket office	*to ekdhotirio isitirion*	το εκδοτήριο εισιτηρίων

Directions

Be prepared when asking directions in Greece! People are a bit more laid back when it comes to direction giving. That 'five minutes' may be 25 minutes; 'near' the post office may mean on the opposite side of town from the post office. The words below will give you a head start.

left	*aristera*	Αριστερά
right	*dheksia*	Δεξιά
straight ahead	*efthia*	Ευθεία
back	*piso*	Πίσω
up	*pano*	Πάνω
down	*kato*	Κάτω
near	*konda*	Κοντά
far	*makria*	Μακριά
under	*apo kato*	Από κάτω
over	*apo pano*	Από πάνω

Traffic & Other Signs

Most road and traffic signs in Greece follow the international convention of using recognisable symbols, so you shouldn't have too much trouble when driving or travelling around. All signs are in both Greek and Latin lettering anyway, though some translations could do with a revision!

alleyway	*parodhos*	Πάροδος
street	*odhos*	Οδός
avenue	*leoforos*	Λεωφόρος
square	*platia*	Πλατεία

ΤΑΜΕΙΟ	CASH DESK (in banks & shops)
ΤΕΛΩΝΕΙΟΝ	CUSTOMS
ΙΑΤΡΕΙΟ	DOCTOR'S SURGERY
ΕΙΣΟΔΟΣ	ENTRY
ΕΞΟΔΟΣ	EXIT
ΑΠΟ	FROM …
ΑΝΔΡΩΝ	GENTLEMEN
ΝΟΣΟΚΟΜΕΙΟ	HOSPITAL
ΠΛΗΡΟΦΟΡΙΕΣ	INFORMATION
ΓΥΝΑΙΚΩΝ	LADIES
ΑΠΑΓΟΡΕΥΕΤΑΙ Η ΣΤΑΘΜΕΥΣΗ	NO PARKING
ΑΠΑΓΟΡΕΥΕΤΑΙ ΤΟ ΚΑΠΝΙΣΜΑ	NO SMOKING
ΑΣΤΥΝΟΜΙΑ	POLICE
ΑΠΑΓΟΡΕΥΕΤΑΙ	PROHIBITED
ΣΥΡΑΤΕ	PULL
ΩΘΗΣΑΤΕ	PUSH
ΣΤΑΣΗ	STOP (Bus/trolley)
ΠΡΟΣ	TO …

Buying Tickets

Ticketing in Greece is gradually joining the computer age, though it is still next to impossible to purchase a rail ticket from anywhere that does not have a rail service, or a boat ticket from an inland city… Bus tickets are commonly computer printed, but rail tickets, more often than not, come on various bits of cardboard. Boat tickets are sometimes computer printed, but few services are linked via online booking systems. Confusion can often be the norm when travelling in Greece.

ΓΡΑΦΕΙΟ ΠΛΙΡΟΦΟΡΙΝ	INFORMATION
ΕΚΔΟΤΗΡΙΑ ΕΙΣΙΤΗΡΙΩΝ	TICKET OFFICE
ΕΙΣΙΤΗΡΙΑ	TICKETS

Excuse me, where is the ticket office?
me sinhorite, pou ine to ekdhotirio isitirion?
Με συγχωρείτε, πού είναι το εκδοτήριο εισιτηρίων;

Where is the information desk?
pou ine to ghrafeio pliroforion?
Πού είναι το γραφείο πληροφοριών;

How much is ...?	*poso kani ...?*	Πόσο κάνει ...;
I'd like ...	*tha ithela ...*	Θα ήθελα ...
one ticket to Mykonos	*ena isitirio ya ti Mikono*	ένα εισιτήριο για τη Μύκονο
two tickets to Mykonos	*dhio isitiria ya ti Mikono*	δυο εισιτήρια για τη Μύκονο
a reservation	*na kliso mya thesi*	να κλείσω μια θέση
single (ticket)	*mono (isitirio)*	μονό (εισιτήριο)
return (ticket)	*(isitirio) me epistrofi*	(εισιτήριο) με επιστροφή
economy	*touristiki thesi*	τουριστική θέση
business class (air)	*dhiakekrimeni thesi*	διακεκριμένη θέση
first class	*proti thesi*	πρώτη θέση

Air

Greece has a well-developed and generally economical air transport system, with flights going to most major and many minor destinations. Most flights originate from, or arrive at, Athens' Hellenikon Airport, while Thessaloniki's Makedonia Airport serves most routes in the northern part of Greece. No smoking is now *de rigueur* on all domestic flights – though many Greeks seem to forget the rule!

ΑΦΙΞΕΙΣ	ARRIVALS
ΠΑΡΑΛΑΒΗ ΑΠΟΣΚΕΥΩΝ	BAGGAGE CLAIM
ΑΝΑΧΩΡΗΣΕΙΣ	DEPARTURE
ΚΑΤΑΣΤΗΜΑ ΑΦΟΡΟΛΟΓΗΤΩΝ	DUTY FREE SHOP
ΓΡΑΦΕΙΟ ΑΠΩΛΕΣΘΕΝΤΩΝ	LOST PROPERTY
ΣΥΝΑΛΛΑΓΜΑ	MONEY EXCHANGE
ΕΓΓΧΟΣ ΔΙΑΒΑΤΗΡΙΩΝ	PASSPORT CONTROL
ΟΤΕ (ΟΡΥΑΝΙΣΜΟΣ ΤΗΛΕΠΙΚΟΙΝΩΝΙΩΝ ΕΛΛΑΔΟΣ)	TELEPHONE OFFICE
ΤΟΥΡΙΣΤΙΚΗ ΑΣΤΥΝΟΜΙΑ	TOURIST POLICE

Is there a flight to (Chania)?
> *iparhi mya ptisi ya ta (Hania)?*

Υπάρχει μια πτήση για τα (Χανιά);

When is the next flight to (Santorini)?
> *pote ine i epomeni ptisi ya ti (Sandorini)?*

Πότε είναι η επόμενη πτήση για τη (Σαντορίνη);

What is the flight number?
pyos ine o arithmos tis ptisis?

Ποιος είναι ο αριθμός της πτήσης;

Where do we check in?
pou paradhinoume tis aposkevez?

Πού παραδίνουμε τις αποσκευές;

When do we have to check in?
pote prepi na paradho-soume tis aposkevez?

Πότε πρέπει να παραδώ-σουμε τις αποσκευές;

One hour/two hours before departure.
mya ora/dhio orez prin apo tin anahorisi

Μια ώρα/δυο ώρες πριν από την αναχώρηση.

Where do you check in luggage?
pou prepi na paradho-soume tis aposkevez?

Πού πρέπει να παραδώ-σουμε τις αποσκευές;

Where do you pick up luggage?
pou prepi na paralavoume tis aposkevez?

Πού πρέπει να παραλάβουμε τις αποσκευές;

Could I have …	mou dhinete, parakalo …	Μου δίνετε, παρακαλώ …
a cup of coffee	enan gafe	έναν καφέ
a cup of tea	ena tsaee	ένα τσάι
a glass of water	ena potiri nero	ένα ποτήρι νερό
a soft drink	ena anapsiktiko	ένα αναψυκτικό
a beer	mya bira	μια μπύρα
a toasted sandwich	ena tost	ένα τοστ

I feel sick.
esthanome aschima   Αισθάνομαι άσχημα.

Bus & Trolleybus

Athens has a well-developed bus service that covers most sub-urbs of Athens, though it can be confusing finding the right bus from the city centre to the suburbs. You buy tickets from ticket kiosks, or small shops and punch them in the machine as you board your bus or trolley. The trolley system is less widespread than the bus system, but all of them pass through central Athens (the only city with trolleys) and their destination is clearly marked (in Greek) on the front of the trolley. They have the same ticketing arrangements as with the buses.

Where is the nearest bus/trolley stop?
pou ine i plisiesteri stasi tou leoforiou/tou trolley?   Πού είναι η πλησιέστερη στάση του λεωφορείου/του τρόλλεϊ;
Which bus goes to Syntagma Square?
pyo leoforio pai stim blatia sindagmatos?   Ποιο λεωφορείο πάει στην Πλατεία Συντάγματος;

Where can I buy a bus ticket?
pou boro naghoraso isitirio Που μπορώ ν'αγοράσω
gia to leoforio? εισιτήριο για το λεωφορείο;
How much does a ticket cost?
poso kani ena isitirio? Πόσο κάνει ένα εισιτήριο;
Please let me know when it is
my stop.
borite na mou pite otan Μπορείτε να μου πείτε όταν
tha ftasoume sti stasi mou θα φτάσουμε στη στάση μου;
How long does it take to get
to the airport?
posi ora kani ya to Πόση ώρα κάνει για το
aerodhromio? αεροδρόμιο;

While on the bus/trolley ...

Excuse me, I'd like to get off!
me sinhorite, thelo Με συγχωρείτε, θέλω
na katevo! να κατεβώ!
Can you tell me where we
are?
borite na mou pite Μπορείτε να μου πείτε
pou imaste? πού είμαστε;
Please tell the driver to stop.
parakalo, peste ston Παρακαλώ, πέστε στον
odhigo na stamatisi οδηγό να σταματήσει.

Train

Greece's train system has always come second to its road transport system – at least in the minds of most Greek travellers – and
has generally been regarded as somewhat inferior and slower. It

is cheaper, admittedly. However, the express Inter City services linking North and South have made travel much more comfortable and are highly recommendable.

Bear in mind: Athens has two railway stations – close to each other – one linking the North – Σταθμός Λαρίσης *(stathmos larisis)* and the other the Peloponnese – Σταθμός Πελοπονήσου *(stathmos peloponisou)*.

ΑΦΙΞΕΙΣ	ARRIVALS
ΑΝΑΧΩΡΗΣΕΙΣ	DEPARTURES

express train	*treno expres*	Τραίνο Εξπρές
international train	*dhiethnes treno*	Διεθνές Τραίνο
intercity train	*treno Inter City*	Τραίνο Ιντερ Σίτυ
kiosk	*periptero*	Περίπτερο
left luggage	*horos aposkevon*	Χώρος αποσκευών
local train	*topiko treno*	Τοπικό Τραίνο
no smoking	*apagorevete*	Απαγορεύεται
	to kapnizma	το Κάπνισμα
railway station	*sidhirodromikos*	Σιδηροδρομικός
	stathmos	Σταθμός
timetable	*dhromologhio*	Δρομολόγιο
train	*treno*	Τραίνο
platform	*apovathra*	Αποβάθρα
waiting room	*ethousa anamonis*	Αίθουσα Αναμονής

I'd like a ticket to
(Thessaloniki).
   thelo ena isitirio ya   Θέλω ένα εισιτήριο για
   (ti Thessaloniki)   (τη Θεσσαλονίκη).

I'd like a first-class ticket.
thelo ena isitirio stim broti thesi

Θέλω ένα εισιτήριο στην πρώτη θέση.

I'd like a second-class ticket.
thelo ena isitirio sti defteri thesi

Θέλω ένα εισιτήριο στη δεύτερη θέση.

I'd like a sleeper.
thelo mya kouketta

Θέλω μια κουκέτα.

Can I make a reservation?
boro na kliso mya thesi?

Μπορώ να κλείσω μια θέση;

I'd like a smoking seat.
tha ithela mya thesi stous kapnizondez

Θα ήθελα μια θέση στους καπνίζοντες.

I'd like a non-smoking seat.
tha ithela mya thesi stous mi kapnizondez

Θα ήθελα μια θέση στους μη καπνίζοντες.

Is there a buffet on the train?
iparhi kilikio sto treno?

Υπάρχει κυλικείο στο τραίνο;

When is the next train to (Corinth)?
pote fevyi to epomeno treno ya (tin Gorintho)?

Πότε φεύγει το επόμενο τραίνο για (την Κόρινθο);

Do I need to change trains?
prepi na allakso trena?

Πρέπει να αλλάξω τραίνα;

What time does the train leave?
ti ora fevyi to treno?

Τι ώρα φεύγει το τραίνο;

What time does the train arrive?
ti ora ftani to treno?

Τι ώρα φτάνει το τραίνο;

Do you take travellers'
cheques?
   dheheste taxidhiotikez
   epitayez?
Δέχεστε ταξιδιωτικές
επιταγές;
How much is the ticket?
   poso kani to isitirio?
Πόσο κάνει το εισιτήριο;

Metro

The expanded Athens Metro system, at the time of writing, was
not in full operation, but some services may be available in the
near future. Currently, the main metro system runs from Kifissia
in Athens' northern suburbs to Piraias, via the centre of Athens
(Omonoia Square). As on the buses and the trolleys, tickets are
purchased beforehand and punched at machines as you enter the
platform. It is a good idea to buy books of tickets, if you intend to
make a lot of use of the system.

Where is the nearest metro
station?
   pou ine o plisiesteros
   stathmos tou Metro?
Πού είναι ο πλησιέστερος
σταθμός του Μετρό;
Where do I purchase a ticket?
   pou prepi naghoraso
   isitirio?
Πού πρέπει ν'αγοράσω
εισιτήριο;
Can you change a 5000
drachma note?
   borite na mou halasete
   ena pendahiliaro?
Μπορείτε να μου χαλάσετε
ένα πενταχίλιαρο;
How much does a ticket to
(Piraias) cost?
   poso kani ena isitirio ya
   (ton Birea)?
Πόσο κάνει ένα εισιτήριο για
(τον Πειραιά);

Please give me a book of tickets.
  sas parakalo, dhoste mou mya dhezmi isitirion
  Σας παρακαλώ, δώστε μου μια δέσμη εισιτηρίων.

Does this train go (to Kifissia)?
  paee, afto to treno (stin Gifisia)?
  Πάει αυτό το τραίνο (στην Κηφισσιά);

Which station is this?
  pyos stathmos ine aftos?
  Ποιος σταθμός είναι αυτός;

Excuse me!
  me sinhorite!
  Με συγχωρείτε!

Taxi

Taxis are cheap and plentiful all over Greece, though getting a taxi in Athens around lunchtime can be impossible. In most places you can book a taxi by phone; otherwise, stand on the nearest street corner and look visible. Many taxis will take sharing passengers: make a note of the amount on the meter as you board and pay the difference only. Taxis from airports, railway stations and ports carry a surcharge. Watch out for taxi 'sharks' at the airport waiting to rip off unsuspecting new arrivals. Keep a close eye on the meter and make sure it is running. The tariff is, by law, on display in the cab: ask to see it, if you are in doubt.

Taxi   *taxi*   Ταξί

Are you free?
  iste eleftheros?
  Είστε ελεύθερος;

I want to go (to the airport).
  thelo na pao (sto aerodhromio)
  Θέλω να πάω (στο αεροδρόμιο).

How much does it cost to go
to the city centre?

poso kani mehri to kendro tis polis?		Πόσο κάνει μέχρι το κέντρο της πόλης;

Could you take me ...?	*borite na me pate ...?*	Μπορείτε να με πάτε ...;
to this address	*safti ti dhiefthinsi*	σ'αυτή τη διεύθυνση
to the airport	*sto aerodhromio*	στο αεροδρόμιο
to the port	*sto limani*	στο λιμάνι
to the railway station	*sto sidhirodhromiko stathmo*	στο σιδηροδρομικό σταθμό
to a cheap hotel	*sena ftino xenodhohio*	σ'ένα φτηνό ξενοδοχείο
to this hotel	*safto to xenodhohio*	σ'αυτό το ξενοδοχείο
to the tourist police	*stin douristiki astinomia*	στην τουριστική αστυνομία
to a doctor	*sena yatro*	σ'ένα γιατρό
to the Canadian Embassy	*stin Kanadheziki prezvia*	στην Καναδέζικη Πρεσβεία
to the main post office	*sto kendriko tahidhromio*	στο κεντρικό ταχυδρομείο

Please slow down!
  pyo argha!   Πιο αργά!
Please stop here.
  parakalo, stamatiste edho   Παρακαλώ, σταματήστε εδώ.
Please wait for a minute.
  perimenete ena lepto   Περιμένετε ένα λεπτό.
How much do I owe you?
  posa sas hrostao?   Πόσα σας χρωτάω;

Please show me the tariff.
   dhixte mou, sas parakalo,
   tin darifa

Δείξτε μου, σας παρακαλώ,
την ταρίφα.

That is too much!
   ine polla!

Είναι πολλά!

I'll report you to the tourist police.
   tha sas katangilo stin
   douristiki astinomia

Θα σας καταγγείλω στην
τουριστική αστυνομία.

Instructions

Is it nearby?
   ine konda?

Είναι κοντά;

Is it far?
   ine makria?

Είναι μακριά;

Can I walk there?
   boro na pao eki me ta
   podhya?

Μπορώ να πάω εκεί με τα
πόδια;

Can you show me on the map?
   borite na mou to dhixete
   sto harti?

Μπορείτε να μου το δείξετε
στο χάρτη;

How many minutes?
   posa lepta?

Πόσα λεπτά;

Go straight ahead.
   piyenete katefthian

Πηγαίνετε κατ'ευθείαν.

Turn left …	*stripste aristera …*	Στρίψτε αριστερά…
Turn right …	*stripste dexia …*	Στρίψτε δεξιά …
at the corner	*sti gonia*	στη γωνία
at the traffic lights	*sta fanaria*	στα φανάρια
at the square	*stim blatia*	στην πλατεία

What … is this?	pyos/pya/pyo … ine?	Ποιος/ποια/ποιο… είναι;
street	dhromos	δρόμος
square	platia	πλατεία
suburb	proastio	προάστειο

Where is (Filellinon) Street?
pou ine h odhos (Fillellinon)? Πού είναι η οδός (Φιλελλήνων);
How far is it to (Nikis) Street?
poso makria ine mehri tin odho (Nikis)? Πόσο μακριά είναι μέχρι την οδό (Νίκης);

Car

Driving in Greece can be a risky affair. Greek drivers have latent suicidal tendencies: the monthly road toll in fatalities bears witness to this. Other than this, driving can be a pleasant experience since traffic is generally lighter than elsewhere in Europe. Petrol prices are generally on a par with other European countries.

Where can I hire a car?
pou boro na nikiaso ena aftokinito? Πού μπορώ να νοικιάσω ένα αυτοκίνητο;
How much does it cost per day?
poso kani tin imera? Πόσο κάνει την ημέρα;
How much does it cost per week?
poso kani tin evdhomadha? Πόσο κάνει την εβδομάδα;
Is insurance included?
ine asfalismeno? Είναι ασφαλισμένο;

Give me … litres of petrol (gasoline).
    dhoste mou, parakalo
    … litra venzinis

Δώστε μου, παρακαλώ,
… λίτρα βενζίνης.

Fill it up.
    yemiste to

Γεμίστε το.

Unleaded petrol (gasoline).
    amolivdhi (venzini)

Αμόλυβδη (βενζίνη).

Can you tell me the way to (Patra)?
    borite na mou dhixete to
    dhromo ya tin Batra?

Μπορείτε να μου δείξετε το δρόμο για (την Πάτρα);

Are we on the right road to (Ioannina)?
    piyenoume kala ya
    ta Yannina?

Πηγαίνουμε καλά για (τα Ιωάννινα);

How far is it to (Kavala)?
    poso makria ine mehri
    tin Gavala?

Πόσο μακριά είναι μέχρι (την Καβάλα);

How far is the next service station?
    poso makria ine mehri to
    epomeno venzinadhiko?

Πόσο μακριά είναι μέχρι το επόμενο βενζινάδικο;

Is it OK to park here?
    boro na parkaro edho?

Μπορώ να παρκάρω εδώ;

Problems

My car has broken down.
    to aftokinito mou nalase

Το αυτοκίνητό μου χάλασε.

Can you help me?
    borite na me voithisete?

Μπορείτε να με βοηθήσετε;

I have lost …	eho hasi …	Εχω χάσει …
my ticket	to isitirio mou	το εισιτήριό μου
my passport	to diavatirio mou	το διαβατήριό μου
my travellers' cheques	tis taxidhiotikez mou epitayez	τις ταξιδιωτικές μου επιταγές
my luggage	tis aposkevez mou	τις αποσκευές μου
my driver's licence	tin adhia odhighiseos	την άδεια οδηγήσεως
my way!	to dhromo!	το δρόμο!

Can you please call the police?

parakalo, borite na tilefoniseta stin astinomia? Παρακαλώ, μπορείτε να τηλεφωνήσετε στην αστυνομία;

Which way is it to the hospital?

pros ta pou vriskete to nosokomio? Προς τα πού βρίσκεται το νοσοκομείο;

Boat

Travelling by boat in Greece can be an exciting yet confusing experience. Greece, being a maritime nation, has boats going to a myriad destinations. They range in quality from local caiques to luxury cruise ships. For most travellers visiting the islands you will be using the regular passenger ferry boats that serve both as a lifeline to the Greek islands and a convenient means of transport for foreign travellers. Piraias serves as the major hub for boats travelling to and from the Aegean and the Mediterranean. Patra and Igoumenitsa serve the Ionian sea and services to and from Italy. Travel by boat is probably the most interesting way to see Greece.

When is the next boat to (Ios)?
pote fevyi to epomeno karavi ya tin Io?
Πότε φεύγει το επόμενο καράβι για την Ιο;

Can I have a single ticket?
mou dhinete ena mono isitirio?
Μου δίνετε ένα μονό εισιτήριο;

Can I have a cabin?
mou dhinete mya kambina?
Μου δίνετε μια καμπίνα;

How much is the cheapest ticket?
poso kani to ftinotero isitirio?
Πόσο κάνει το φτηνότερο εισιτήριο;

How many hours is it to (Folegandros)?
posez orez ine mehri ti Foleghandro?
Πόσες ώρες είναι μέχρι (τη Φολέγανδρο);

Does the boat stop at (Milos)?
stamatai to karavi sti Milo?
Σταματάει το καράβι (στη Μήλο);

What time does the boat depart/arrive?
ti ora fevyi/ftani to karavi
Τι ώρα φεύγει/φτάνει το καράβι;

Where does the boat depart from?
apo pou fevyi to karavi
Από πού φεύγει το καράβι;

Can I book a ticket today?
boro na kopso isitirio simera?
Μπορώ να κόψω εισιτήριο σήμερα;

Is there a restaurant on board?
to karavi ehi estiatorio?
Το καράβι έχει εστιατόριο;

GETTING AROUND

Do you accept Eurailpass?
   dheheste Eurailpass?   Δέχεστε EURAILPASS;
Do you have student discounts?
   dhinete fititikez ekptosis?   Δίνετε φοιτητικές εκπτώσεις;

Paperwork

Greeks are great bureaucrats and you may be asked to fill in a form at some stage of your visit to Greece. Usually someone will be on hand to help you, but it helps to know what it is you are filling in. The following terms are some of the more common ones that you will come across.

Name	*onoma*	Ονομα.
Surname	*eponimo*	Επώνυμο
Father's name	*onoma patros*	Ονομα πατρός
Address	*dhiefthinsi*	Διεύθυνση
Date of birth	*imerominia yenniseos*	Ημερομηνία γεννήσεως
Place of birth	*topos yenniseos*	Τόπος γεννήσεως
Age	*ilikia*	Ηλικία
Sex	*fillo*	Φύλλο
Religion	*thriskevma*	Θρήσκευμα
Profession	*epangelma*	Επάγγελμα
Passport Number	*arithmos diavatiriou*	Αριθμός Διαβατηρίου
Identity Card	*taftotita*	Ταυτότητα
Residence Permit	*adhya paramonis*	Αδεια Παραμονής
Birth Certificate	*pistopiitiko yenniseos*	Πιστοποιητικό Γεννήσεως
Driver's Licence	*adhia odhighiseos*	Αδεια Οδηγήσεως
Car registration certificate	*adhya kikloforias aftokinitou*	Αδεια Κυκλοφορίας Αυτοκινήτου
Car registration number	*arithmos kikloforias aftokinitou*	Αριθμός Κυκλοφορίας Αυτοκινήτου
Duty Stamp (always required on official documents)	*hartosimo*	Χαρτόσημο

Some Useful Phrases

See also Emergencies, page 202.

I want to contact my
Embassy.
   thelo na epikinoniso me
   tim Brezvia mou
     Θέλω να επικοινωνήσω με
     την Πρεσβεία μου.

I need a lawyer.
   hriazome dhikighoro
     Χρειάζομαι δικηγόρο.

I have no money.
   dhen eho lefta
     Δεν έχω λεφτά.

I need help.
   hriazome voithia
     Χρειάζομαι βοήθεια.

I want to go home!
   thelo na pao stim
   batridha mou!
     Θέλω να πάω στην
     πατρίδα μου!

GETTING AROUND

Accommodation

Finding accommodation in Greece is never really much of a problem, unless you are in Greece in the middle of July when it seems everyone is looking for somewhere to stay. Accommodation ranges from spartan beach camping to luxury hotels: you will always find something to suit your budget. Very often you'll be met at tourist locations by locals wishing to offer you rooms – δωμάτια *(dhomatya)*. These are often good options and convenient ways to meet Greek families. English is usually widely spoken, but if you have some Greek, you probably have that extra edge. The following section should see you through most common situations.

Finding Accommodation

Can you tell me where there's ...?	*borite na mou pite pou iparhi ...?*	Μπορείτε να μου πείτε πού υπάρχει ... ;
a good hotel	*ena kalo xenodohio*	ένα καλό ξενοδοχείο
a cheap hotel	*ena ftino xenodohio*	ένα φτηνό ξενοδοχείο
a room for the night	*ena dhomatio ya mya vradhya*	ένα δωμάτιο για μια βραδυά
a youth hostel	*enas xenonas neotitos*	ένας ξενώνας νεότητος
an information bureau	*ena ghrafio pliroforion*	ένα γραφείο πληροφοριών
a camping site	*ena kamping*	ένα κάμπιγκ

81

At the Hotel

Very commonly you will be asked to surrender your passport when you check into a hotel, or even private rooms. This is both for the purposes of registration and for security, though in the latter case you are entitled to ask for your passport back after registration is completed – especially since you will probably need it for identification when changing travellers' cheques or even purchasing tickets. Offer another document, like a driver's licence, or an identity card, if this causes difficulties.

Checking In

I'd like a ...	*thelo ena ...*	Θέλω ένα ...
single room	*mono dhomatio*	μονό δωμάτιο
double room	*dhiplo dhomatio*	διπλό δωμάτιο
room for ...	*dhomatio ya ...*	δωμάτιο για ...
people	*atoma*	άτομα
room with a	*dhomatio me dous*	δωμάτιο με ντους
shower and toilet	*ke toualetta*	και τουαλέττα

How much is the	*poso kani to*	Πόσο κάνει το
room ...?	*dhomatio ...*	δωμάτιο ...
per night	*ti vradhya*	τη βραδυά
for ... nights	*ya ... vradhyez*	για ... βραδνές
per week	*tin evdhomadha*	την εβδομάδα

Is breakfast included?
simberilamvani ke   Συμπεριλαμβάνει και
proïno?   πρωϊνό;
What time do I have to
check out?
ti ora prepi na figho apo   Τι ώρα πρέπει να φύγω από
to dhomatio?   το δωμάτιο;

Is there a telephone in the room?

ehi tilefono sto dhomatio?　Εχει τηλέφωνο στο δωμάτιο;

Is there a TV in the room?

ehi tileorasi sto dhomatio?　Εχει τηλεόραση στο δωμάτιο;

What is the room number?

ti arithmo ehi to dhomatio?　Τι αριθμό έχει το δωμάτιο;

Can I see the room?

boro na dho to dhomatio?　Μπορώ να δω το δωμάτιο;

Can I have my passport please?

mou dhinete, parakalo, to diavatirio mou?　Μου δίνετε, παρακαλώ το διαβατήριό μου;

Can I give you my driver's licence?

boro na sas dhoso tin adhya odhighiseos?　Μπορώ να σας δώσω την άδεια οδηγήσεως;

Requests & Complaints

I'll take the room.

tha to paro to dhomatio　Θα το πάρω το δωμάτιο.

The room is too small.

to dhomatio ine mikro　Το δωμάτιο είναι μικρό.

Can you show me another room?
borite na mou dhixete allo dhomatio?
Μπορείτε να μου δείξετε άλλο δωμάτιο;

Thanks, but it's not suitable.
sas efharisto, alla dhe mou kani
Σας ευχαριστώ, αλλά δε μου κάνει.

Can I have some more blankets?
mou dhinete ki allez kouvertez
Μου δίνετε κι άλλες κουβέρτες;

Is there hot water available?
ehi zesto nero?
Εχει ζεστό νερό;

The shower doesn't work.
to dous dhe dhoulevi
Το ντους δε δουλεύει.

There is no hot water.
dhen ehi zesto nero
Δεν έχει ζεστό νερό.

The TV is broken.
halase i tileorasi
Χάλασε η τηλεόραση.

I can't open the window.
dhem boro nanikso to parathiro
Δε μπορώ να ανοίξω το παράθυρο.

The pillow is too hard.
to maxilari ine poli skliro
Το μαξιλάρι είναι πολύ σκληρό.

Can I leave my valuables here?
boro nafiso ta andikimena axias mazi sas?
Μπορώ ν'αφήσω τα αντικείμενα αξίας μαζί σας;

Can I have …?	*mou dhinete …?*	Μου δίνετε …?
my key	*to klidhi mou*	το κλειδί μου
my luggage	*tis aposkevez mou*	τις αποσκευές μου
the account	*to loghariasmo*	το λογαριασμό

Some Useful Words & Phrases

It's too cold.
  kani poli krio — Κάνει πολύ κρύο.

It's too hot.
  kani poli zesti — Κάνει πολύ ζέστη.

It's very noisy.
  kani poli thorivo — Κάνει πολύ θόρυβο.

I'd like to make a phone call.
  thelo na kano ena tilefonima — Θέλω να κάνω ένα τηλεφώνημα.

air conditioning	*klimatizmos*	κλιματισμός
bed	*krevati*	κρεββάτι
cupboard	*doulapi*	ντουλάπι
door	*porta*	πόρτα
electrical socket	*briza*	μπρίζα
fan	*anemistiras*	ανεμιστήρας
heating	*thermansi*	θέρμανση
light	*fos*	φως
lock	*klidharia*	κλειδαριά
radiator	*kalorifer*	καλοριφέρ
sheets	*sendonia*	σεντόνια
shutters	*pandzouria*	παντζούρια
soap	*sapouni*	σαπούνι
tap (faucet)	*vrisi*	βρύση
toilet	*toualetta*	τουαλέττα
toilet paper	*harti iyias*	χαρτί υγείας

towel	*petseta*	πετσέτα
wash basin	*niptiras*	νιπτήρας
window	*parathiro*	παράθυρο

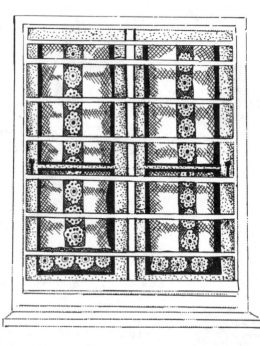

Checking Out

I'm checking out ... *fevgho* ... Φεύγω ...
    today   *simera*   σήμερα
    tonight   *apopse*   απόψε
    tomorrow   *avrio*   αύριο

Can I leave my luggage here?
    mporo nafiso tis   Μπορώ ν'αφήσω τις
    aposkevez mou edho   αποσκευές μου εδώ;
Can you call me a taxi?
    borite na tilefonisete   Μπορείτε να τηλεφωνήσετε
    ya ena taxi?   για ένα ταξί;

Laundry

Do-it-yourself laundrettes are not very common in Greece: there
are one or two in Athens and Thessaloniki. Drycleaners, on the
contrary, abound. You are better off doing it yourself at your
hotel or guesthouse. When the weather is warm, your clothes
will be dry in no time.

Is there a washing machine
I can use?
    iparhi plindirio?   Υπάρχει πλυντήριο;
Can I have an iron?
    mou dhinete ena sidhiro?   Μου δίνετε ένα σίδηρο;
Can I have some washing
powder?
    mou dhinete ligho   Μου δίνετε λίγο
    aporipandiko?   απορρυπαντικό;
How do I switch it on?
    pos anighi?   Πώς ανοίγει;

88   Laundry

The washing machine doesn't
work.
   dhe dhoulevi to plindirio   Δε δουλεύει το πλυντήριο.
Is there a drycleaners nearby?
   iparhi katharistirio konda?   Υπάρχει καθαριστήριο κοντά;
Do you have a needle and
thread?
   ehete velona ke klosti?   Εχετε βελόνα και κλωστή;

Some Useful Words

'bum bag'	*tsanda banana*	τσάντα μπανάνα
alarm clock	*xipnitiri*	ξυπνητήρι
backpack	*sakkidhyo*	σακκίδιο
mattress	*stroma*	στρώμα
padlock	*louketo*	λουκέτο
penknife	*souyas*	σουγιάς
plug adaptor	*adapter*	αντάπτερ
scissors	*psalidhi*	ψαλίδι
sleeping bag	*ipnosakkos*	υπνόσακκος
suitcase	*valitsa*	βαλίτσα
toiletry gear	*toualetika*	τουαλετικά
youth hostel card	*karta Xenona Neotitos*	κάρτα Ξενώνα Νεότητος
zip	*fermouar*	φερμουάρ

Around Town

At the Bank

As a visitor to Greece, your interaction with Greek banks will commonly be limited to currency exchange and possibly receipt of bank transfers from your home country. Most banks have a separate currency exchange counter where you will usually be served quickly and efficiently. Larger cities and tourist resorts often have dedicated exchange facilities and in some places you will now find automated currency exchange machines. Receiving money from overseas is usually not too much of a problem, but when buying foreign currency, or sending money overseas, you often run up against the formidable Greek bureaucratic machine. Always have your passport with you when visiting the bank.

Here are some of the signs you'll commonly see in and around banks.

ΤΡΑΠΕΖΑ	BANK
ΣΥΝΑΛΛΑΓΜΑ	CURRENCY EXCHANGE
ΤΑΜΕΙΟ	CASHIER
ΧΡΗΜΑΤΟΘΥΡΙΔΑ	AUTOMATIC CASH MACHINE
ΔΙΕΥΘΥΝΤΗΣ	MANAGER

Do you change travellers'
cheques?
  exaryironete taxidhiotikez   Εξαργυρώνετε ταξιδιωτικές
  epitayez?   επιταγές;

90

travellers' cheques	*taxidhiotikez epitayez*	ταξιδιωτικές επιταγές
personal cheques	*prosopikez epitayez*	προσωπικές επιταγές
Eurocheques	*evrotsek*	Ευρωτσέκ
US$	*amerikanika dhollaria*	αμερικάνικα δολλάρια
UK£	*lirez anglias*	λίρες Αγγλίας
Australian $	*afstralezika dhollaria*	αυστραλέζικα δολλάρια
Canadian $	*kanadhezika dhollaria*	καναδέζικα δολλάρια
New Zealand $	*neozilandhika dhollaria*	νεοζηλανδικά δολλάρια

I'd like to change this money
into drachmas.
   tha ithela na kano afta ta   Θα ήθελα να κάνω αυτά
   lefta se dhrahmez   τα λεφτά σε δραχμές.

How many drachmas will that
be?
   posez dhrahmez tha ine?   Πόσες δραχμές θα είναι;

Do you take a commission?
   pernete promithya?   Παίρνετε προμήθεια;

Could you please write that
down?
   borite na mou to grapsete?   Μπορείτε να μου το γράψετε;

What is the exchange rate?
   poso pai to sinallaghma?   Πόσο πάει το συνάλλαγμα;

Can I have some money
transferred to here?
   boro na metafero   Μπορώ να μεταφέρω
   hrimata edho?   χρήματα εδώ;

How long will it take?
poson gero tha pari?   Πόσον καιρό θα πάρει;

Have you received my money yet?
pirate akoma ta hrimata mou?   Πήρατε ακόμα τα χρήματά μου;

I'd like to buy some local money.
tha ithela naghoraso xeno sinallaghma   Θα ήθελα ν'αγοράσω ξένο συνάλλαγμα.

Could I speak to the manager?
boro na miliso sto dhiefthindi?   Μπορώ να μιλήσω στο διευθυντή;

At the Post Office

Greek post offices are the focus of most mailing activity in any town: this is because most Greeks don't seem to like using mailboxes and always go the post office to mail their letters. The Greek Postal Service (ΕΛΤΑ) is generally reliable and economi-

cal for domestic mail, but mail to and from overseas has some-times suffered from a bad reputation – delays, losses and strikes. If you are sending parcels overseas, take them in unwrapped, so that they can be checked. You can usually change travellers' cheques at post offices – useful on weekends, or when the banks are closed. You can often send faxes from post offices too.

Here are some signs you will see in and around post offices.

ΤΑΧΥΔΡΟΜΕΙΟ	POST OFFICE
ΕΠΕΙΓΟΝΤΑ	EXPRESS MAIL
ΣΥΣΤΗΜΕΝΑ	REGISTERED MAIL
ΓΡΑΜΜΑΤΟΣΗΜΑ	STAMPS
ΔΕΜΑΤΑ	PARCELS
ΕΝΤΑΛΜΑΤΑ	MONEY ORDERS
ΤΗΛΕΦΑΞ	FAX SERVICE
ΕΝΤΑΥΘΑ	LOCAL MAIL

Where is the post office?
   pou ine to tahidhromio?   Πού είναι το ταχυδρομείο;
What time does the post
office open?
   ti ora anighi to   Τι ώρα ανοίγει το
   tahidhromio?   ταχυδρομείο;
Where is the nearest
letterbox?
   pou ine to plisiestero   Που είναι το πλησιέστερο
   ghrammatokivotio?   γραμματοκιβώτιο;
I'd like to send this letter to
(Australia).
   tha ithela na stilo afto to   Θα ήθελα να στείλω αυτό το
   ghramma stin (Afstralia)   γράμμα στην (Αυστραλία).

AROUND TOWN

How much does a stamp cost?
poso kani ena
ghrammatosimo?

Πόσο κάνει ένα
γραμματόσημο;

Could I have a stamp for
(South Africa)?
mou dhinete ena ghramma-
tosimo ya (ti Notia Afriki)?

Μου δίνετε ένα γραμματόσημο
για (τη Νότια Αφρική);

I want to send this letter …
thelo na stilo afto to
ghramma …

Θέλω να στείλω αυτό το
γράμμα …

I want to send this parcel …
thelo na stilo afto to
dhema …

Θέλω να στείλω αυτό το
δέμα …

I want to send this postcard by
regular mail.
thelo na stilo afti
tin garta apla

Θέλω να στείλω αυτή
την κάρτα απλά.

by regular mail	*apla*	απλά
registered	*sistimena*	συστημένα
by air mail	*aeroporikos*	αεροπορικώς
by express mail	*katepighon*	κατ'επείγον

I want to send a fax message.
thelo na stilo ena fax

Θέλω να στείλω ένα φαξ.

How much does it cost per
page?
poso kani i selidha?

Πόσο κάνει η σελίδα;

Where is the poste restante?
pou ine to post restan?

Πού είναι το Ποστ Ρεστάν;

Do I have any mail?
eho kanena ghramma?

Εχω κανένα γράμμα;

Here are some more useful post office-related terms …

aerogramme	*aeroghramma*	αερόγραμμα
envelope	*fakelos*	φάκελος
padded bag	*enischimenos fakelos*	ενισχυμένος φάκελος
pen	*stilo*	στυλό
postal code	*tahidhromikos kodikas*	ταχυδρομικός κώδικας
postal order	*tahidhromiki epitayi*	ταχυδρομική επιταγή
receipt	*apodhiksi*	απόδειξη
sticky tape	*kollitiki tenia*	κολλητική ταινία
string	*spangos*	σπάγγος
stamp	*ghrammatosimo*	γραμματόσημο
wrapping paper	*xarti tilighmatos*	χαρτί τυλίγματος
writing paper	*harti alliloghrafias*	χαρτί αλληλογραφίας

Telephone

The Greek telephone system, operated by the Greek Telecommunications Organisation (OTE, pronounced *o-tay)* is not yet a state-of-the-art operation. Domestic calls can be notoriously unreliable, but international calls can be exceptionally efficient. Calls can be made from the OTE offices, from street kiosks *(periptera)* and, increasingly from 'telecard' phones. Coin-operated boxes are becoming more and more rare – they never were popular in Greece. Calls are expensive by US, Canadian, Australian and New Zealand standards, but bear in mind you might be able to use the 'Call Home' facility with your own country's 'Phone Card'. To make a call from a kiosk – the easiest option – just pick up the phone and dial. Your call details will be recorded on a meter in the kiosk. At the OTE office you will be allocated a booth: make your call and pay afterwards at the cash desk. With TELECARDS, simply insert and dial.

ΤΗΛΕΦΩΝΟ	TELEPHONE
ΤΗΛΕΚΑΡΤΑ	TELECARD
ΟΡΓΑΝΙΣΜΟΣ	GREEK
ΤΗΛΕΠΙΚΟΙΝΩΝΙΩΝ	TELECOMMUNICATIONS
ΕΛΛΑΔΟΣ (ΟΤΕ)	ORGANISATION (OTE)
ΤΑΜΕΙΟ	CASHIER

I'd like to make a call to
(Ireland).
   thelo na tilefoniso stin   Θέλω να τηλεφωνήσω στην
   (Irlandhia)   (Ιρλανδία).
How much does it cost per
minute?
   poso kani to lepto?   Πόσο κάνει το λεπτό;
How much do I owe you?
   posa sas hrostao?   Πόσα σας χρωστάω;
I got the wrong number!
   pira lathos arithmo!   Πήρα λάθος αριθμό.
We were cut off.
   mas dhiekopsan   Μας διέκοψαν.
Can I make a reverse call to
(Scotland)?
   mporo na hreoso to   Μπορώ να χρεώσω το
   tilefonima sti (skotia)?   τηλεφώνημα στη (Σκωτία);
What is the country code for
(Singapore)?
   pyos ine o dhiethnis   Ποιος είναι ο διεθνής κώδικας
   kodhikas ya ti (Singapouri)?   για τη (Σιγκαπούρη);

What is the overseas access code?

   pyos ine o dhiethnis   Ποιος είναι ο διεθνής
   kodhikas kliseos?   κώδικας κλήσεως;

The number is engaged.

   milai   Μιλάει.

Do you have a telephone directory?

   ehete tilefoniko katalogho?   Εχετε τηλεφωνικό κατάλογο;

Every country has its own way of answering phone calls. When you call a Greek phone number you will commonly hear the following responses …

Εμπρός!	*embros!*	Hello!
Λέγετε ...	*leyete ...*	(lit) 'You may speak ...'
Ναι ...	*ne*	Yes ...

When it is your turn to speak in Greek, any of the following expressions should help you through the initial stages.

This is Mr/Ms ...
   milai o kirios/i kiria ...   Μιλάει ο κύριος/η κυρία ...
I'd like to speak to Mr/Ms ...
   tha ithela na miliso   Θα ήθελα να μιλήσω
   ston girio/stin giria ...   στον κύριο/στην κυρία ...
Could I speak with someone
who speaks English?
   boro na miliso se kapyon   Μπορώ να μιλήσω με κάποιον
   pou xeri anglika?   που ξέρει Αγγλικά;
Could I have extension
number ... ?
   mou dhinete ton esoteriko Μου δίνετε τον εσωτερικό
   arithmo ...?   αριθμό ...;
Could you speak more loudly?
   milate pyo dhinata,   Μιλάτε πιο δυνατά
   parakalo?   παρακαλώ;
I'm sorry, I can't hear you.
   sighnomi, dhe sas akouo   Συγγνώμη, δε σας ακούω.
I'll call again.
   tha sas xanaparo   Θα σας ξαναπάρω.

Sightseeing

With a history as long and varied as that of Greece, there is no lack of sights to see. You probably wouldn't see all there is to see in a lifetime. Take your time, plan your itinerary and enjoy! Use the following expressions to get around and to keep one step ahead of the crowds.

Excuse me, which is the way
to the Acropolis?
 me sinhorite, pyos ine o   Με συγχωρείτε, ποιος είναι ο
 dhromos ya tin akropoli?   δρόμος για την Ακρόπολη;

the Acropolis	*tin akropoli*	την Ακρόπολη
the National Museum	*to Ethniko Mousio*	το Εθνικό Μουσείο
the ruins	*ta arhea*	τα αρχαία
the art gallery	*tim binakothiki*	την πινακοθήκη
the cathedral	*ti mitropoli*	τη μητρόπολη
the church	*tin ekklisia*	την εκκλησία
the tourist office	*to touristiko ghrafio*	το τουριστικό γραφείο
the monastery	*to monastiri*	το μοναστήρι

How much is the entry fee?
 poso kani i isodhos?   Πόσο κάνει η είσοδος;
Do you have a student
discount?
 dhinete fititiki ekptosi?   Δίνετε φοιτητική έκπτωση;
Is there an English-speaking
guide?
 iparhi anglofonos xenaghos?   Υπάρχει αγγλόφωνος ξεναγός;
May I take photographs?
 boro na vghalo   Μπορώ να βγάλω
 fotoghrafiez?   φωτογραφίες;
What are the opening hours?
 pyez orez anighi?   Ποιες ώρες ανοίγει;
What time does it close?
 ti ora klini?   Τι ώρα κλείνει;

AROUND TOWN

It's ...	*ine* ...	Είναι ...
beautiful	*oreo*	ωραίο
impressive	*endiposiako*	εντυπωσιακό
interesting	*endhiaferon*	ενδιαφέρον
magnificent	*iperoho*	υπέροχο
strange	*paraxeno*	παράξενο

Entertainment

Greeks are big on nightlife. Recent government legislation to curb Greeks' nocturnal entertainment fever is sure to meet with stiff resistance. Greeks' idea of a 'night out' is at the 'bouzoukia' where you can hear popular top-name musicians and pay top price for your food and drinks. Younger Greeks love discos and just 'hanging out' with each other. The cafeterias are popular spots to hang out and have a 'frappé' – iced nescafé drunk through a straw and which seems to last for ever. Eating out, of course, is big business too – from local eateries to smart restaurants: the choice is yours. There is no lack of theatres, cinemas and other cultural activities wherever you go. Life in Greece begins, so they say, after midnight!

I'd like to go ...	*tha ithela na pao ...*	Θα ήθελα να πάω...
to the 'bouzouki'	*sta bouzoukia*	στα μπουζούκια
to a traditional restaurant	*sena paradhosiako estiatorio*	σ' ένα παραδοσιακό εστιατόριο
to a movie	*sto sinema*	στο σινεμά
to a night club	*sena night club*	σ' ένα νάιτ κλαμπ
to a Greek play	*sena elliniko theatriko ergho*	σ' ένα ελληνικό θεατρικό έργο
to a disco	*sena disco*	σ' ένα ντίσκο
to a quiet bar	*sena isiho bar*	σ' ένα ήσυχο μπαρ
to a soccer match	*sena podhosferiko aghona*	σ' ένα ποδοσφαιρικό αγώνα
to a concert	*se mya sinavlia*	σε μια συναυλία
to an (Italian) restaurant	*sena (italiko) estiatorio*	σ' ένα (Ιταλικό) εστιατόριο
to the beach	*sti thalassa*	στη θάλασσα

AROUND TOWN

Do you have a table free?
  ehete kanena elefthero trapezi? Εχετε κανένα ελεύθερο τραπέζι;
Is there live music?
  ehi zondani mousiki? Εχει ζωντανή μουσική;
Is the movie in English?
  to ergho ine sta anglika? Το έργο είναι στα Αγγλικά;
Could I have two tickets?
  mou dhinete dhio isitiria? Μου δίνετε δυο εισιτήρια;
Is there an entrance fee?
  ehi timi isodhou? Εχει τιμή εισόδου;
How much is it?
  poso kani? Πόσο κάνει;

Please bring me ...	*mou fernete ...*	Μου φέρνετε ...
a beer	*mya bira*	μια μπύρα
an ouzo	*ena ouzo*	ένα ούζο
a whisky	*ena whisky*	ένα ουίσκυ;
a plate of snacks	*mya pyatella me mezedhes*	μια πατέλλα με μεζέδες
the bill	*to loghariazmo*	το λογαριασμό

Signs

Most signs – especially in tourist areas – will be in Greek and in any number of other languages. It's more fun to be able to decipher the Greek, so here are a few of the ones you are likely to come across.

ΕΣΤΙΑΤΟΡΙΟ	RESTAURANT
ΤΑΒΕΡΝΑ	TAVERNA
ΤΙΜΟΚΑΤΑΛΟΓΟΣ	MENU
ΣΙΝΕΜΑ	CINEMA
ΘΕΑΤΡΟ	THEATRE
ΜΠΑΡ	BAR
ΚΑΦΕΤΕΡΙΑ	CAFETERIA
ΖΑΧΑΡΟΠΛΑΣΤΕΙΟ	CAKE SHOP
ΚΑΦΕΝΕΙΟ	KAFENIO (GREEK COFFEE SHOP)
ΟΥΖΕΡΙ	OUZERI (OUZO BAR)
ΕΙΣΟΔΟΣ	ENTRY
ΕΞΟΔΟΣ	EXIT
ΤΟΥΑΛΕΤΤΕΣ	TOILETS
ΠΛΑΖ	BEACH

Some Useful Phrases

Everyone's idea of entertainment or nightlife is different, but the following useful words and phrases will always be useful, wherever you end up.

AROUND TOWN

I need a taxi.
  hriazome ena taxi   Χρειάζομαι ένα ταξί.

Take me to (the Lykavettos) hotel.
  me piyenete sto xenodohio (Likavitto)   Με πηγαίνετε στο ξενοδοχείο (Λυκαβηττό).

I had a good time!
  perasa poli orea!   Πέρασα πολύ ωραία!

Thank you for your company.
  efharisto ya tin barea   Ευχαριστώ για την παρέα.

See you tomorrow.
  tha sas dho avrio   Θα σας δω αύριο.

Can I take you home?
  boro na sas pao sto spiti sas?   Μπορώ να σας πάω στο σπίτι σας;

I have a bad headache.
  eho meghalo ponokefalo   Εχω μεγάλο πονοκέφαλο.

In the Country

Weather

In Greece the weather is not always hot and humid, as many are led to believe. In the summer it can, of course, be unbearably hot, but the mountains are usually much cooler. In winter there can be very heavy snowfalls all over the mainland, with some fine skiing for those who like winter sports. Like anywhere else, talking about the weather is always a good ice-breaker when meeting people.

It's hot.	*kani zesti*	Κάνει ζέστη.
It's humid.	*ehi ighrasia*	Εχει υγρασία.
It's cold.	*kani krio*	Κάνει κρύο.
It's chilly	*kani psihra*	Κάνει ψύχρα.
It's windy.	*fisaee*	Φυσάει.
It's snowing.	*hionizi*	Χιονίζει.
It's raining.	*vrehi*	Βρέχει.
It's sunny.	*ehi ilio*	Εχει ήλιο.

summer	*kalokeri*	καλοκαίρι
autumn	*fthinoporo*	φθινόπωρο
winter	*himonas*	χειμώνας
spring	*anixi*	άνοιξη

The weather is ...	*o keros ine ...*	Ο καιρός είναι ...
superb	*iperohos*	υπέροχος
beautiful	*oreos*	ωραίος
idyllic	*idhanikos*	ιδανικός

perfect	*telios*	τέλειος
awful	*aschimos*	άσχημος
dreadful	*apesios*	απαίσιος

Some Useful Expressions

You may not always understand what is being said to you, but try the following anyway and see what response you get.

What will the weather be like today?
   ti kero tha kani simera?   Τι καιρό θα κάνει σήμερα;
What is the temperature?
   ti thermokrasia ehoume?   Τι θερμοκρασία έχουμε;
I love the heat!
   pos maresi i zesti!   Πώς μ'αρέσει η ζέστη!

IN THE COUNTRY

Some Useful Words

storm	*thiella*	θύελλα
downpour	*kateyidha*	καταιγίδα
rain	*vrohi*	βροχή
hail	*halazi*	χαλάζι
ice	*paghos*	πάγος
dawn	*ximeroma*	ξημέρωμα
sunset	*iliovasilema*	ηλιοβασίλεμα

Along the Way

The following expressions should help you if you are exploring on your own.

Please tell me the way to ...	*parakalo, borite na mou dhixete to dhromo ya ...*	Παρακαλώ, μπορείτε να μου δείξετε το δρόμο για ...
How far is it to ...?	*poso makria ine mehri ?*	Πόσο μακριά είναι μέχρι ...;
the ancient theatre	*to arheo theatro*	το αρχαίο θέατρο
the beach	*tim baralia*	την παραλία
the castle	*to kastro*	το κάστρο
the cave	*to spileo*	το σπήλαιο
the cemetery	*to nekrotafio*	το νεκροταφείο
the forest	*to dhasos*	το δάσος
the gorge	*ti haradhra*	τη χαράδρα
the lake	*ti limni*	τη λίμνη
the river	*to potami*	το ποτάμι
the mountain	*to vouno*	το βουνό
the spring	*to pighadhi*	το πηγάδι
the village	*to horio*	το χωριό
the waterfall	*tous kataraktes*	τους καταρράκτες;

How many hours will it take?
posez orez tha kani?   Πόσες ώρες θα κάνει;

Is it easy to find?
tha to vro efkola?   Θα το βρω εύκολα;

Are there signs?
iparhoun tambellez?   Υπάρχουν ταμπέλλες;

How many kilometres?
posa hiliometra?   Πόσα χιλιόμετρα;

Directions

Which way?	*pros ta pou?*	Προς τα πού;
Left.	*aristera*	Αριστερά.
Right.	*dhexia*	Δεξιά.
Straight ahead.	*efthia*	Ευθεία.
Back.	*piso*	πίσω.
to the east	*anatolika*	ανατολικά
to the west	*dhitika*	δυτικά
to the north	*voria*	βόρεια
to the south	*notia*	νότια

Animals

Greece has a lot of countryside where animals roam freely, but, like elsewhere in the world, they are threatened by human encroachment and pollution, and are considered by many people 'fair game' for hunting. Wolves, fierce sheep dogs and the odd snake are more likely encountered in the mountains, whereas your main problems by the beach are stinging insects.

Are there any wild animals?
   iparhoun aghria zoa?   Υπάρχουν άγρια ζώα;
Are they dangerous?
   ine epikindhina?   Είναι επικίνδυνα;

Here are some common animal names.

animal	*zo-o*	ζώο
bear	*arkoudha*	αρκούδα
cat	*ghata*	γάτα
deer	*elafi*	ελάφι
dog	*skili*	σκυλί

IN THE COUNTRY

donkey	*ghaïdharos*	γάιδαρος
fox	*alepou*	αλεπού
frog	*vatrahos*	βάτραχος
goat	*katsiki*	κατσίκι
hare	*laghos*	λαγός
horse	*alogho*	άλογο
lizard	*savra*	σαύρα
mule	*moulari*	μουλάρι
rabbit	*kouneli*	κουνέλι
shark	*karharias*	καρχαρίας
sheep	*provato*	πρόβατο
sheepdog	*mandroskilo*	μαντρόσκυλο
wolf	*likos*	λύκος

Birds

bird	*pouli*	πουλί
eagle	*ayetos*	αετός
hawk	*yeraki*	γεράκι
kingfisher	*alkiona*	αλκυόνα
owl	*koukouvaya*	κουκουβάγια
partridge	*perdhika*	πέρδικα
pelican	*pelekanos*	πελεκάνος
pheasant	*fasianos*	φασιανός
pigeon	*peristeri*	περιστέρι
seagull	*ghlaros*	γλάρος
stork	*leleki*	λελέκι

Insects & Other Creatures

I've been stung by ...	*me tsimbise ...*	Με τσίμπησε ...
I've been bitten by ...	*me dhangose ...*	Με δάγκωσε ...
a bee	*mya melissa*	μια μέλισσα

IN THE COUNTRY

a hornet	*mya meghali sfika*	μια μεγάλη σφήκα
a insect	*ena endomo*	ένα έντομο
a jellyfish	*mya tsouhtra*	μια τσούχτρα
a mosquito	*ena kounoupi*	ένα κουνούπι
a scorpion	*enas skorpios*	ένας σκορπιός
a sea-urchin	*enas ahinos*	ένας αχινός
a snake	*ena fidhi*	ένα φίδι
a wasp	*mya sfika*	μια σφήκα

It hurts.
    ponaee   Πονάει.
It is swollen.
    ehi pristi   Εχει πρηστεί.
I feel dizzy.
    esthanomai zaladha   Αισθάνομαι ζαλάδα.

Plants

There are some wonderful flowers and plants in Greece. Respect nature and leave it as you would like to find it.

bush	*thamnos*	θάμνος
carnation	*gharifallo*	γαρύφαλλο
cypress	*kiparissi*	κυπαρίσσι
flower	*louloudhi*	λουλούδι
grass	*hortari*	χορτάρι

mountain tea	*tsaee tou vounou*	τσάι του βουνού
olive tree	*elya*	ελιά
oregano	*righani*	ρίγανη
palm	*finika*	φοίνικα
pine	*pefko*	πεύκο
plane	*platanos*	πλάτανος
plant	*fito*	φυτό
rose	*triandafillo*	τριαντάφυλλο
thyme	*thimari*	θυμάρι
tree	*dhendro*	δέντρο

IN THE COUNTRY

Camping

Greece is well endowed with attractive and well-equipped camping sites, so you should never have trouble finding somewhere to pitch your tent. Should you find it necessary to 'bush camp', respect nature and others nearby. Leave your site as you found it.

Where is the camping ground?
   pou ine to camping?   Πού είναι το κάμπιγκ;
Can I camp here?
   boro na kataskinoso edho?   Μπορώ να κατασκηνώσω εδώ
How much is it per night?
   poso kani ti vradhya?   Πόσο κάνει τη βραδιά;
Where is the office?
   pou ine to grafio?   Πού είναι το γραφείο;
Where are the toilets?
   pou ine i toualettez?   Πού είναι οι τουαλέττες;
Can we light a fire?
   boroume nanapsoume fotia?   Μπορούμε ν'ανάψουμε φωτιά;
Where can I get water?
   pou boro na paro nero?   Πού μπορώ να πάρω νερό;

Some Useful Words

bridge	*yefiri*	γεφύρι
cloud	*sinnefo*	σύννεφο
cobbled path	*kalderimi*	καλντερίμι
field	*horafi*	χωράφι
hill	*lofos*	λόφος
hut	*kaliva*	καλύβα
map	*hartis*	χάρτης
marsh	*valtos*	βάλτος
meadow	*livadhi*	λειβάδι
refuge	*katafiyio*	καταφύγιο
stream	*riaki*	ρυάκι
tent	*skini*	σκηνή
trail	*monopati*	μονοπάτι
wall	*tihos*	τοίχος
water fountain	*vrisi*	βρύση

IN THE COUNTRY

Food

With plenty of natural produce both from the land and the sea, and blessed with a temperate Mediterranean climate, Greek cuisine is an amalgam of all that is good in the Mediterranean and surrounding lands. Eating in Greece is a highlight of any visit and Greek restaurants can now be found in most corners of the globe for when you get that feeling of nostalgia for your Greek trip.

At the Restaurant

Many Greek restaurants tend to be informal affairs and you can usually go along to the kitchen to see what is on display. Otherwise, the menus tend to be in Greek and, usually, English. Bread and water are always placed on the table. Service charge is normally included, though it is common courtesy to leave a small tip.

Do you have a table for two?
   ehete trapezi ya dhio atoma?   Εχετε τραπέζι για δυο άτομα;
Can I see the menu please?
   boro na dho to menou?   Μπορώ να δω το μενού;
Do you have a menu in English?
   ehete menou sta anglika?   Εχετε μενού στα Αγγλικά;
Can I look in the kitchen?
   boro na kitaxo stin gouzina?   Μπορώ να κοιτάξω στην κουζίνα;
What do you recommend?
   ti sinistate?   Τι συνιστάτε;

What is this/that?
ti ine afto/ekino?

Τι είναι αυτό/εκείνο;

I would like …
tha ithela …

Θα ήθελα …

I want the same as his/hers.
thelo to idhio me to dhiko tou/tis

Θέλω το ίδιο με το δικό του/της.

Can I try that?
boro na dhokimaso ekino

Μπορώ να δοκιμάσω εκείνο.

I just want a Greek salad.
thelo mya horiatiki salata mono

Θέλω μια χωριάτικη σαλάτα μόνο.

Could we have some house wine?
mas fernete krasi tou maghaziou?

Μας φέρνετε κρασί του μαγαζιού;

I am (very) hungry.
pinao (poli)

Πεινάω (πολύ).

I am (very) thirsty.
dhipsao (poli)

Διψάω (πολύ).

Could we have the bill?
mas fernete to loghariazmo?

Μας φέρνετε το λογαριασμό;

Vegetarian Meals

Greeks are not normally 'declared' vegetarians but some eat 'vegetarian' food as a fact of life. While Greeks tend to be big meat eaters, many rural dishes are based on vegetables and pulses only and provide some of the tastiest meals that you will find.

I am a vegetarian.
   ime hortofaghos   Είμαι χορτοφάγος.
Do you serve vegetarian food?
   servirete fayito ya   Σερβίρετε φαγητό για
   hortofaghous?   χορτοφάγους;

I'd like …	*tha ithela …*	Θα ήθελα …
some vegetables	*merika lahanika*	μερικά λαχανικά
bean soup	*fasoladha*	φασολάδα
lentil soup	*fakez*	φακές
a salad	*mya salata*	μια σαλάτα

I don't eat dairy products.
   dhen dro-o ghalaktokomika Δεν τρώω γαλακτοκομικά
   proïonda   προϊόντα.

Breakfast

Breakfast is generally not a big affair in Greece. Most Greeks make do with a Greek coffee and maybe a piece of bread and cheese. As a visitor, you will normally be able to find what you are used to. A popular one is a simple coffee and *voutiro-meli*, βούτυρο-μέλι – bread, butter and honey.

I'd like some breakfast please.
   tha ithela ena proïno,   Θα ήθελα ένα πρωινό,
   parakalo   παρακαλώ.

FOOD

Could I have some bread,
butter and honey?
  mou fernete ena   Μου φέρνετε ένα
  voutiro meli?   βούτυρο-μέλι;

Do you have ... ?   *mipos ehete ...?*   Μήπως έχετε ... ;
  boiled eggs   *avgha vrasta*   αυγά βραστά
  cereals   *dhimitriaka*   δημητριακά
  cold milk   *krio ghala*   κρύο γάλα
  croissants   *krouassan*   κρουασσάν
  fried eggs   *avgha tighanita* αυγά τηγανιτά
  a Greek coffee *ena elliniko kafe* ένα ελληνικό καφέ

FOOD

marmalade/jam   *marmeladha*   μαρμελάδα
a Nescafé (instant) *ena neskafe*   ένα νεσκαφέ
an omelette   *mya omeleta*   μια ομελέττα
tea   *tsaee*   τσάι

Lunch

Lunch tends to be the major meal of the day and is eaten after work any time after, say, 1 pm. People in a hurry may eat at a *mayirio*, μαγειρείο – a restaurant with homemade food and an emphasis on informality, or at any number of fast food outlets *fastfoudadhika,* φαστφουντάδικα. Home cooking is the usual option.

Do you know a good restaurant?
   mipos xerete ena kalo estiatorio?   Μήπως ξέρετε ένα καλό εστιατόριο;

I'd like something light.
   thelo kati elafri   Θέλω κάτι ελαφρύ.

I'd like some seafood.
   thelo thalassina   Θέλω θαλασσινά.

I prefer traditional Greek food.
   protimo tim baradhosiaki elliniki kouzina   Προτιμώ την παραδοσιακή ελληνική κουζίνα.

Here are some common menu terms that you'll find on most menus.

Σούπες	*soupez*	soups
Ορεκτικά	*orektika*	starters/appetisers
Στιφάδο	*stifadho*	stew
Ψαρικά	*psarika*	fish dishes
Ζυμαρικά	*zimarika*	pasta dishes
Κρέατα	*kreata*	meat dishes
Μεζέδες	*mezedhez*	snacks
Χόρτα	*horta*	greens
Πιλάφι	*pilafi*	rice

Τηγανιτ–ός/ή/ό	*tighanit–os/i/o*	fried
Βραστ–ός/ή/ό	*vrast–os/i/o*	boiled
Ψητ–ός/ή/ό	*psit–os/i/o*	roast
Γεμιστ–ός/ή/ό	*yemist–os/i/o*	stuffed
Της ώρας	*tis oras*	to order
Της σχάρας	*tis scharas*	grilled

Dinner

Dinner tends to be a more elaborate affair, if taken at all. However many Greeks make do with a light snack in the evening, if they are not eating out. If they do eat out, it will commonly be at a family *taverna,* ταβέρνα, a *psistarya,* ψησταριά specialising in meats, or perhaps at a *pizzeria,* πιτσαρία which are very popular options. Meals eaten out often start late – after 10 pm – and end late. Other than in smarter big city restaurants, it is not usually necessary to book.

Could we try your speciality?
   boroume na dhokimasoume   Μπορούμε να δοκιμάσουμε
   to spesialite sas?   το σπεσιαλιτέ σας;

Could you bring us a good local wine?
   mas fernete ena kalo   Μας φέρνετε ένα καλό
   topiko krasi?   τοπικό κρασί;

We need some more bread.
   hriazomaste ki allo psomi.   Χρειαζόμαστε κι άλλο ψωμί.

Do you have a chair for the baby?
   ehete kareklaki ya to   Εχετε καρεκλάκι για το
   moro?   μωρό;

Where are the toilets?
   pou ine i toualetez?   Που είναι οι τουαλέτες;

FOOD

Can we put two tables
together?
 boroume na valoume dhio   Μπορούμε να βάλουμε δυο
 trapezia mazi?   τραπέζια μαζί;
The meal was delicious.
 to fayito itan nostimotato   Το φαγητό ήταν νοστιμότατο.

Staples
Greek staples naturally reflect the local produce. Olive oil is the
mainstay of cooking mediums, while potatoes, tomatoes, bread,
cheese, olives and vegetables and fruits in season will always
find their way onto a Greek table. Here are the names of some of
the basic staples.

beans	*fasolia*	φασόλια
bread	*psomi*	ψωμί
cheese	*tiri*	τυρί
flour	*alevri*	αλεύρι
lentils	*fakez*	φακές
olive oil	*eleoladho*	ελαιόλαδο
olives	*elyez*	ελιές
pasta	*zimarika*	ζυμαρικά
rice	*rizi*	ρύζι
salt	*alati*	αλάτι

Breads
Bread plays a very important role in the diet of a Greek. Very few
Greeks would eat a meal without bread and it is always present
on the table. Bread is usually bought daily from the local baker.
Western-style sliced bread can be bought at supermarkets, though
it tends to be rather bland. Bear in mind there are two words for

FOOD

bread: the everyday word ψωμί *(psomi)* and the purist word άρτος *(artos)* which you will often see at the baker.

bread	*psomi/artos*	ψωμί – άρτος
croissant	*krouassan*	κρουασσάν
dark (brown) bread	*mavro psomi*	μαύρο ψωμί
dry biscuit	*paximadhi*	παξιμάδι
loaf	*frandzola*	φραντζόλα
roll	*psomaki*	ψωμάκι
rusk	*frighanya*	φρυγανιά
rye bread	*psomi sikaleos*	ψωμί σικάλεως
wheat bread	*sitarenio psomi*	σιταρένιο ψωμί

Bread is bought by weight, so …

A kilo of brown (dark) bread.
  ena kilo mavro psomi   Ενα κιλό μαύρο ψωμί.
Half a kilo of rye (bread).
  miso kilo sikaleos   Μισό κιλό σικάλεως.

Dairy Produce

Although there is plenty of milk to be had in Greece, milk is not as popular in the average Greek's diet as it is in, say, northern Europe. Many Greek children have been brought up on sweetened condensed milk instead of 'real' milk, though things are changing. Feta cheese is a mainstay of most Greeks' diets and is usually found in a traditional 'Greek' salad.

butter	*voutiro*	βούτυρο
cheese	*tiri*	τυρί
cottage cheese	*mizithra*	μιζήθρα
cream	*krema*	κρέμα
feta (sheep's milk cheese)	*feta*	φέτα
Gruyère	*ghraviera*	γραβιέρα
hard cheese like parmesan	*kefalotiri*	κεφαλοτύρι
margarine	*margharini*	μαργαρίνη
milk	*ghala*	γάλα
whipped cream	*sandiyi*	σαντιγύ
yellowish sheep's milk cheese	*kaseri*	κασέρι

FOOD

Appetisers

aubergine dip	*melidzanosalata*	μελιτζανοσαλάτα
cheese pie	*tiropita*	τυρόπιττα
fish roe dip	*taramosalata*	ταραμοσαλάτα
fried feta cheese	*saghanaki*	σαγανάκι
meat balls	*keftedhakya*	κεφτεδάκια
octopus	*ohtapodhi*	οχταπόδι
potato & garlic dip	*skordhalya*	σκορδαλιά
sausages	*loukanika*	λουκάνικα
shrimps	*gharidhez*	γαρίδες
spicy yoghurt dip	*dzadziki*	τζατζίκι
spinach pie	*spanakopita*	σπανακόπιττα
squid	*kalamaria*	καλαμάρια
stuffed vine leaves	*dolmadhez*	ντολμάδες

Soup

Not a huge variety here, but very tasty!

bean soup	*fasoladha*	φασολάδα
chicken soup	*kotosoupa*	κοτόσουπα
(Easter) entrail soup	*mayiritsa*	μαγειρίτσα
egg & lemon soup	*avgholemono*	αυγολέμονο
fish soup	*psarosoupa*	ψαρόσουπα
lentil soup	*faki soupa*	φακή σούπα
tripe soup	*patsas*	πατσάς
vegetable soup	*hortosoupa*	χορτόσουπα

Meat

Standard fare, plus some offal.

beef	*vodhino*	βοδινό
chicken	*kotopoulo*	κοτόπουλο

FOOD

chops	*brizolez*	μπριζόλες
entrails	*endosthia*	εντόσθια
hare	*laghos*	λαγός
kidney	*sikoti*	σηκώτι
lamb	*arni*	αρνί
liver	*nefra*	νεφρά
mince	*kimas*	κιμάς
mixed entrails on the spit	*kokoretsi*	κοκορέτσι
pork	*hirino*	χοιρινό
sausage	*loukaniko*	λουκάνικο
souvlaki (meat cubes on skewers)	*souvlaki*	σουβλάκι
spare ribs	*paeedhakya*	παϊδάκια
veal	*moschari*	μοσχάρι
yiros (combined meats on skewers)	*yiros*	γύρος

Seafood

Sadly, overfishing in the Mediterranean has meant that fish tends to be pretty expensive. But it is still popular and there is a wide variety.

bream	*lithrini*	λιθρίνι
cod	*bakalyaros*	μπακαλιάρος
cuttlefish	*soupya*	σουπιά
lobster	*astakos*	αστακός
mullet	*barbouni*	μπαρμπούνι
mussels	*midhya*	μύδια
oysters	*stridhya*	στρύδια
prawns	*garidhez*	γαρίδες
salmon	*solomos*	σολωμός

FOOD

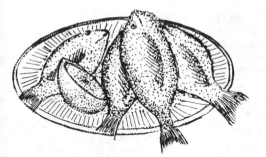

sole	*ghlosa*	γλώσσα
sea pike	*zarghana*	ζαργάνα
swordfish	*xifias*	ξιφίας
trout	*pestrofa*	πέστροφα
whitebait	*maridha*	μαρίδα

Salads

Salads are an important part of a Greek meal, but Greeks rarely eat them on their own as you may do in your country. Boiled 'wild greens' salads are very popular and much appreciated.

cabbage salad	*lahanosalata*	λαχανοσαλάτα
lettuce salad	*maroulosalata*	μαρουλοσαλάτα
potato salad	*patatasalata*	πατατασαλάτα
Russian salad	*rossiki salata*	ρώσσικη σαλάτα
tomato & cucumber salad	*angourodomata-salata*	αγγουροντοματα-σαλάτα
village (Greek) salad	*horiatiki salata*	χωριάτικη σαλάτα
wild greens salad	*horta*	χόρτα

FOOD

Vegetables

Some vegetables are referred to previously, but here is a more comprehensive list. Vegetables eaten on their own in an oil-based sauce are very popular. Dishes made this way are know as λαδερά *(ladhera)* – vegetables in oil.

artichokes	*anginarez*	αγγινάρες
aubergines (eggplants)	*melidzanez*	μελιτζάνες
beetroot	*pandzari*	παντζάρι
cabbage	*lahano*	λάχανο
cauliflower	*kounoupidhi*	κουνουπίδι
courgettes (zucchini)	*kolokithakya*	κολοκυθάκια
green beans	*fasolakya*	φασολάκια
leeks	*prasa*	πράσσα
lettuce	*marouli*	μαρούλι
okra (ladies fingers)	*bamiez*	μπάμιες
onions	*kremidhya*	κρεμμύδια
peas	*arakas*	αρακάς
peppers (capsicums)	*piperyez*	πιπεριές
potatoes	*patatez*	πατάτες
spinach	*spanaki*	σπανάκι
tomatoes	*domatez*	ντομάτες

Common Dishes

Here are some common dishes you will encounter as you travel across Greece and Cyprus.

μουσακάς
  mousakas – mousakas (shepherd's pie). Layers of potatoes and aubergines, mincemeat sauce topped with béchamel sauce.
παστίτσιο
  pastitsio – macaroni pie. Similar to mousakas, but with macaroni instead of potatoes and aubergines.

στιφάδο
stifadho – stew. Usually done in red-wine sauce and very
    tasty.
φασολάδα
fasoladha – bean soup
γιουβαρλάκια
youvarlakya – mincemeat balls in rice, egg and lemon soup
κεφτέδες
keftedhez – fried mincemeat balls

aubergines 'imam'	*melitzanez imam*	μελιτζάνες ιμάμ
hamburgers	*biftekia*	μπιφτέκια
kebab	*tas kebab*	τας κεμπάμπ
lamb on the spit	*arni souvlas*	αρνί σούβλας
ragoût potatoes	*patatez yahni*	πατάτες γιαχνί
rissoles	*soudzoukakya*	σουτζουκάκια
spaghetti with meat sauce	*makaronia me kima*	μακαρόνια με κιμά
spinach with rice	*spanakorizo*	σπανακόρυζο
stuffed aubergines	*papoutsakia*	παπουτσάκια
stuffed (peppers or tomatoes)	*yemista*	γεμιστά
veal casserole	*moschari stifadho*	μοσχάρι στιφάδο

Condiments

basil	*vasiliko*	βασιλικό
mint	*dhiozmos*	δυόσμος
oregano	*righani*	ρίγανη
parsley	*maeedanos*	μαϊντανός
pepper	*piperi*	πιπέρι
salt	*alati*	αλάτι

FOOD

Fruit

Fresh fruit in season usually constitutes dessert after a Greek meal.

apples	*mila*	μήλα
apricots	*verikoka*	βερίκοκα
bananas	*bananez*	μπανάνες
cantaloupe (melon)	*peponi*	πεπόνι
cherries	*kerasia*	κεράσια
figs	*sika*	σύκα
grapes	*stafilia*	σταφύλια
oranges	*portokalia*	πορτοκάλια
peaches	*rodhakina*	ροδάκινα
watermelon	*karpouzi*	καρπούζι

Desserts & Sweets

While desserts tend to be mainly fresh fruit, sweets are in another league again. If you have a sweet tooth, you can indulge in your passion at any time of the day with the following sweets.

μπακλαβάς
baklavas – baklava. Sections of flaky pastry filled with honey and nuts.
μπουγάτσα
boughatsa – bougatsa. Custard cream.
Φρούτα της εποχής
frouta tis epohis – fruit in season. Whatever is going at the time.
χαλβάς
halvas – halva. In Greece this is a kind of semolina cake.
καταΐφι
kataifi – kataïfi. A syrupy sweet made of shredded filo pastry, honey and almonds.

custard pie	*ghalaktoboureko*	γαλακτομπούρεκο
honey macaroons	*melomakarona*	μελομακάρονα
honey puffs	*loukoumadhez*	λουκουμάδες
rice pudding	*rizoghalo*	ρυζόγαλο
shortbread biscuits	*kourabiedhez*	κουραμπιέδες
Turkish delight	*loukoumi*	λουκούμι
turnovers	*dhiplez*	δίπλες

Drinks

Drinking alcohol in Greece is always done to the accompaniment of some food, whether it be a full meal or simply snacks – μεζέδες *(mezedhez)*. Drinking coffee is as popular as ever but the once ubiquitous Greek coffee seems to be giving way to the the frappé (whipped iced Nescafé) that is preferred by the young. Tea drinking tends to be restricted to medicinal purposes.

FOOD

Nonalcoholic

capuccino	*capoutsino*	καπουτσίνο
espresso	*espresso*	εσπρέσσο
Greek coffee	*ellinikos kafes*	ελληνικός καφές
iced coffee	*frappé*	φραππέ
mineral water	*metalliko nero*	μεταλλικό νερό
mountain tea	*tsaï tou vounou*	τσάι του βουνού
Nescafé (instant)	*nescafé*	νεσκαφέ
soft drink	*anapsiktiko*	αναψυκτικό
tea	*tsaï*	τσάι

Alcoholic

ούζο
  ouzo – ouzo. Popular local drink with a strong aniseed
  flavour.
ρετσίνα
  retsina – retsina. Local drink with a resin flavour.
ρακί
  raki – raki. A strong spirit distilled from grain and usually
  with a strong aniseed flavour.

beer	*bira*	μπύρα
bottled ...	... *se boukali*	... σε μπουκάλι
draught ...	... *hima*	... χύμα
cognac	*konyak*	κονιάκ
whisky	*whisky*	ουίσκυ
wine	*krasi*	κρασί
dry wine	*xiro krasi*	ξηρό κρασί
house wine	*krasi hima*	κρασί χύμα
red wine	*kokkino krasi*	κόκκινο κρασί
sweet wine	*ghliko krasi*	γλυκό κρασί
white wine	*aspro krasi*	άσπρο κρασί

FOOD

Some Useful Phrases

Compliments to the chef!
sinharitiria sto mayira!   Συγχαρητήρια στο μάγειρα!

Can I have the recipe?
mou dhinete ti sindayi?   Μου δίνετε τη συνταγή;

Bon appétit!
kali orexi!   Καλή όρεξη!

I am full.
hortasa   Χόρτασα.

Cheers!
stin iya sas!   Στην υγειά σας!

Bottoms up!
aspro pato!   Ασπρο πάτο!

Enough!
ftani!   Φτάνει!

I'd like to make a toast …
thelo na kano mya proposi…   Θέλω να κάνω μια πρόποση …

FOOD

Shopping

If you like shopping when you are on holiday, you will enjoy yourself in Greece. Apart from fixed-price department stores and supermarket items, you will probably get away with a modicum of good-natured bargaining for most tourist purchases. Credit cards are widely accepted – though not always preferred – and quite often foreign currency can be used to make purchases.

Shops tend to open early and close for lunch and siesta at about 2 pm. Apart from Mondays and Wednesdays, they open again in the afternoon, at about 5, and close at about 9 pm. Main shops are normally closed on Sundays, though you can always find local groceries open for your basic food needs. The ubiquitous kiosks, *periptera*, περίπτερα have an amazing range of products from condoms to newspapers; beer to shampoo.

Shopping is not as cheap as it used to be. In fact you will find many items may be more expensive than at home. Luxury taxes have been removed from most electrical goods, but cars are still very expensive in Greece.

Shop Signs
Half the fun of learning Greek is in recognising signs and learning how to say them. Things can be a tad confusing in Greece: the sign on the shop is not always what people call the shop. This is the most visible example of Greece's diglossy – 'demotic' Greek versus 'purist Greek'. The following table will show you what you will see on the shop front, what it means and what Greeks really call the shop.

Purist Greek ...	It Means ...	Greeks Say ...
ΑΡΤΟΠΟΙΕΙΟΝ	BAKERY	ΦΟΥΡΝΟΣ
ΚΡΕΟΠΩΛΕΙΟΝ	BUTCHER	ΧΑΣΑΠΙΚΟ
ΓΑΛΑΚΤΟΠΩΛΕΙΟΝ	DAIRY SHOP	ΓΑΛΑΤΑΔΙΚΟ
ΙΧΘΥΟΠΩΛΕΙΟΝ	FISH SHOP	ΨΑΡΑΔΙΚΟ
ΟΠΩΡΟΠΩΛΕΙΟΝ	GREENGROCER	ΜΑΝΑΒΙΚΟ
ΠΑΝΤΟΠΩΛΕΙΟΝ	GROCERY	ΜΠΑΚΑΛΙΚΟ
ΥΠΟΔΗΜΑΤΟΠΩΛΕΙΟΝ	SHOE SHOP	ΠΑΠΟΥΤΣΑΔΙΚΟ
ΚΑΤΑΣΤΗΜΑ	SHOP	ΜΑΓΑΖΙ
ΥΠΕΡΑΓΟΡΑ	SUPERMARKET	ΣΟΥΠΕΡ-ΜΑΡΚΕΤ

Making a Purchase
Bargaining

There are some unwritten rules about bargaining that any travel-ler needs to bear in mind. The principles are much the same in Greece as anywhere else where bargaining is common, except perhaps that they are not always stringently adhered to.

Once you start bargaining with a potential vendor, there is a tacit understanding that you are seriously interested in purchas-ing, so don't start bargaining unless you really want an item. The secret is to be good-natured and to estimate the point at which

SHOPPING

you can get your item at the price you want without making the seller lose interest. At the end of the day, the seller always 'wins', but bargaining is more than just shopping, it is a social interaction, an integral part of life in the Mediterranean. Approach it this way and you will enjoy your shopping expeditions more!

I'd like to buy …	*tha ithela naghoraso …*	Θα ήθελα ν'αγοράσω …
Please show me …	*borite na mou dhixete …*	Μπορείτε να μου δείξετε …
one of these	*ena ap'afta*	ένα απ'αυτά
one of those	*ena ap'ekina*	ένα από εκείνα
a souvenir	*kati ya souvenir*	κάτι για σουβενίρ
a present	*kati ya doro*	κάτι για δώρο
Greek music	*paradhosiaki elliniki mousiki*	παραδοσιακή ελληνική μουσική
Greek handicrafts	*elliniki hirotehnia*	ελληνική χειροτεχνία

How much does it cost?
poso kani?   Πόσο κάνει;

That's too expensive.
ine poli akrivo   Είναι πολύ ακριβό.

Can you make me a better price?
mou kanete mya kaliteri timi?   Μου κάνετε μια καλύτερη τιμή;

I am just looking.
aplos kitazo   Απλώς κοιτάζω.

I want something …	*thelo kati …*	Θέλω κάτι …
a bit cheaper	*pyo ftino*	πιο φτηνό
a bit smaller	*pyo mikro*	πιο μικρό
a bit bigger	*pyo meghalo*	πιο μεγάλο

of better quality	*kaliteris pyotitas*	καλύτερης ποιότητας
of a different colour	*dhiaforetikou hromatos*	διαφορετικού χρώματος

Does it have a guarantee?
  ehi engi-isi?   Εχει εγγύηση;
Can you wrap it please?
  *borite na mou to tilixete   Μπορείτε να μου το τυλίξετε
  parakalo?*   παρακαλώ;
Can you send it to (Hong
Kong)?
  *borite na to stilete sto   Μπορείτε να το στείλετε στο
  (Hong Kong)?*   (Χογκ Κογκ);
How much all together?
  posa kanoun ola mazi?   Πόσα κάνουν όλα μαζί;

Do you take … ?	*pernete …?*	Παίρνετε … ;
credit cards	*pistotikez kartez*	πιστωτικές κάρτες
foreign currency	*xeno sinallaghma*	ξένο συνάλλαγμα
Eurocheques	*evrotsek*	Ευρωτσέκ

That's all, thanks.
  tipote allo, efharisto   Τίποτε άλλο, ευχαριστώ.
OK, I'll take it.
  endaxi, tha to paro   Εν τάξει, θα το πάρω.
Sorry, it's not quite what I
wanted.
  *sighnomi, dhen ine akrivos   Συγγνώμη, δεν είναι ακριβώς
  afto pou ithela*   αυτό που ήθελα.
Thank you for your time!
  *sas efharisto ya tin   Σας ευχαριστώ για την
  ora sas!*   ώρα σας!

Souvenirs

OK, armed with the basic requests listed above, you can now try your skill at purchasing the item you want. Here is a list of some of the more common souvenir items.

bag/handbag	*tsanda*	τσάντα
cassette	*kasetta*	κασέττα
CD	*see dee*	CD
embroidery	*kendita*	κεντητά
hat	*kapello*	καπέλλο
key ring	*brelok*	μπρελόκ
playing cards	*trapoula*	τράπουλα
postcard	*karta*	κάρτα
pottery	*keramika*	κεραμικά
purse/wallet	*portofoli*	πορτοφόλι
record	*dhiskos*	δίσκος
statue	*aghalma*	άγαλμα
sunglasses	*yalya iliou*	γυαλιά ηλίου
T-shirt	*blouzaki*	μπλουζάκι
tea towel	*petsetaki*	πετσετάκι
tray	*dhiskos*	δίσκος
worry beads	*komboloy*	κομπολόι

Buying Greek Music

One of the most lasting and rewarding souvenirs of any trip is buying some music to take home with you. What could be better to remember those endless meals under the stars …? For the un-initiated, it can be difficult to buy the music that you may often hear. The 'tourist music' trade may only offer you a watered-down version of what you heard. The real music will be found in Greek music stores. Here is a short guide to what you might hear, where to find it and how to ask for it. Bear in mind that composers are often just as important as the singers, so you can find album titles under composers' names as well as under singers' names.

Some of the more popular Greek singers are:

Αλκηστη Πρωτοψάλτη	Alkisti Protopsalti
Δημήτρης Κοντολάζος	Dimitris Kondolazos
Δημήτρης Μητροπάνος	Dimitris Mitropanos
Ελευθερία Αρβανιτάκη	Eleftheria Arvanitaki
Ελένη Βιτάλη	Eleni Vitali
Γεώργος Νταλάρας	Georgos Dalaras
Γλυκερία	Glykeria
Χάρις Αλεξίου	Haris Alexiou
Κυριαζής	Kyriazis
Μανώλης Μητσιάς	Manolis Mitsias
Στέλιος Καζαντίδης	Stelios Kazantzidis
Βασίλης Παπακωνσταντίνου	Vasilis Papakonstantinou
Γιάννης Πάριος	Yannis Parios

Some of the more popular Greek composers are the following:

Μίκης Θεοδωράκης	Mikis Theodorakis
Γιάννης Μαρκόπουλος	Yannis Markopoulos
Μάνος Χατζιδάκις	Manos Hatzidakis
Γιάννης Σπανός	Yannis Spanos
Ελένη Καραΐνδρου	Eleni Karaindrou
Απόστολος Καλδάρας	Apostolos Kaldaras
Δήμος Μούτσης	Dimos Moutsis
Δημήτρης Λάγιος	Dimitris Lagios
Μάνος Λοΐζος	Manos Loizos

The best place to buy music is in the specialist music stores where there are no tourists in sight. Every city and town has a large number of them, both big and small. Cassettes are the most popular medium – but watch out for forgeries. Make sure yours has the official quality seal. CDs are growing in popularity and vinyl is not yet dead in Greece. Prices for CDs tend to be more expensive than at home, but bear in mind you may find that Greek CD you wanted in your Greek music store in Melbourne or Montreal at a cheaper price!

I'd like the latest album ...	*tha ithela to telefteo album ...*	Θα ήθελα το τελευταίο άλμπουμ...
by George Dalaras	*tou Dalara*	του Νταλάρα
by Haris Alexiou	*tis Alexiou*	της Αλεξίου

Do you have any good ... music?	*mipos ehete kali ... mousiki?*	Μήπως έχετε καλή ... μουσική;
Cretan	*Kritiki*	Κρητική
Thracian	*Thrakiotiki*	Θρακιώτικη

Macedonian	*Makedhoniki*	Μακεδονική
easy listening	*elafrolaeeki*	ελαφρολαϊκή
ecclesiatical	*ekklisiastiki*	εκκλησιαστική
folk	*dhmotiki*	δημοτική
Greek pop music	*elliniki pop*	ελληνική ποπ
rembetika	*rembetiki*	ρεμπέτικη

Can you recommend a good
album?
   borite na mou sinistisete   Μπορείτε να μου συνιστήσετε
   ena kalo album?   ένα καλό άλμπουμ;
Can I listen to it?
   boro na to akouso?   Μπορώ να το ακούσω;
That's great! I'll take it.
   poli oreo, tha to paro   Πολύ ωραίο! Θα το πάρω.

Clothing

belt	*zoni*	ζώνη
bikini	*bikini*	μπικίνι
blouse	*blouza*	μπλούζα
bra	*soutien*	σουτιέν
dress	*fousta*	φούστα
jacket	*sakakki*	σακάκκι
jeans	*blue-tzin*	μπλου-τζήν
underpants	*vraki*	βρακί
overcoat	*palto*	παλτό
parka	*boufan*	μπουφάν
pyjamas	*pidzamez*	πυτζάμες
raincoat	*adhiavroho*	αδιάβροχο
scarf	*kaskol*	κασκόλ
shirt	*poukamiso*	πουκάμισο
shoes	*papoutsia*	παπούτσια

SHOPPING

skirt	*foustani*	φουστάνι
socks	*kaltsez*	κάλτσες
stockings	*kalson*	καλσόν
suit	*koustoumi*	κουστούμι
sweater	*pullover/blouza*	πουλόβερ/μπλούζα
swimming wear	*mayo*	μαγιώ
tie	*ghravata*	γραβάτα
trousers	*pandeloni*	παντελόνι
underwear	*esorouha*	εσώρουχα

Materials

For the more adventurous, here are the Greek names of various types of material.

cotton	*vamvakero*	βαμβακερό
woollen	*mallino*	μάλλινο
nylon	*nylon*	νάυλον
velvet	*veloudhino*	βελούδινο
leather	*dhermatino*	δερμάτινο
linen	*lino*	λινό
corduroy	*veloudho kotle*	βελούδο κοτλέ
satin	*saten*	σατέν
silk	*metaxoto*	μεταξωτό
polyester	*polyester*	πολυέστερ

Toiletries & Pharmaceuticals

Many basic toiletries can be bought at περίπτερα *(periptera)* or at supermarkets. Chemists tend to deal mainly in pharmaceuticals and don't necessarily have the same variety of goods as in Australia, or other similar countries. Many drugs that would normally require prescription in your country can be bought over the counter at pharmacies.

At the Chemist

I want something for …	*thelo kati ya …?*	Θέλω κάτι για …;
a cold	*ena kriologhima*	ένα κρυολόγημα
a cough	*ena viha*	ένα βήχα
a headache	*ena ponokefalo*	ένα πονοκέφαλο
insect bites	*tsimbimata apo endoma*	τσιμπήματα από έντομα
hay fever	*allerghiko sinahi*	αλλεργικό συνάχι
travel sickness	*naftia taxidhiou*	ναυτία ταξιδιού
diarrhoea	*efkiliotita*	ευκοιλιότητα
sunburn	*iliokama*	ηλιόκαμα
un upset stomach	*piraghmeno stomahi*	πειραγμένο στομάχι

Can I have …?	*mou dhinete …?*	Μου δίνετε … ;
some aspirin	*aspirini*	ασπιρίνη
a bandage	*ena epidhezmo*	ένα επίδεσμο
a syringe	*mya siringa*	μια σύριγγα
some cotton wool	*vamvaki*	βαμβάκι
some Band-aids	*merika lefkoplast*	μερικά λευκοπλάστ
a packet of condoms	*ena paketo profilaktika*	ένα πακέτο προφυλακτικά
some sanitary towels	*ena paketo serviettez*	ένα πακέτο σερβιέττες
some disinfectant	*apolimandiko*	απολυμαντικό
a thermometer	*ena thermometro*	ένα θερμόμετρο
some cough drops	*pastilyez ya viha*	παστίλιες για βήχα

Do I need a prescription?
mipoz hriazome sindayi?   Μήπως χρειάζομαι συνταγή;

At the Supermarket or Kiosk

aftershave	*mya andhriki kolonia*	μια ανδρική κολώνια
cologne	*mya kolonia*	μια κολώνια
comb	*mya htena*	μια χτένα
conditioner	*mallaktiko mallion*	μαλλακτικό μαλλιών
deodorant	**ena** *aposmitiko*	ένα αποσμητικό
insect repellant	*apothotiko endomon*	αποθωτικό εντόμων
razor	*ena xirafi*	ένα ξυράφι
soap	*ena sapouni*	ένα σαπούνι
shampoo	*ena sambouan*	ένα σαμπουάν
shaving cream	*krema xirizmatos*	κρέμα ξυρίσματος
sponge	*ena sfoungari*	ένα σφουγγάρι
sunblock	*krema iliou*	κρέμα ηλίου
talcum powder	*poudhra*	πούδρα
packet of tissues	*ena paketo hartomandila*	ένα πακέτο χαρτομάντηλα
toothbrush	*mya odhondovourtsa*	μια οδοντόβουρτσα
tube of toothpaste	*mya odhondokrema*	μια οδοντόκρεμα
pair of tweezers	*ena tsimbidhaki*	ένα τσιμπιδάκι

Stationery & Publications

Newspapers are often displayed for public perusal at kiosks and newsagents and often attract large crowds – especially when there is a political scandal, or a favourable soccer report. English language periodicals can be found at kiosks in most tourist areas, though in smaller towns, you may have to go to the newsagent. Writing materials can usually be bought at bookstores, as well as at kiosks.

Is there a newsagent nearby?
iparhi praktorio   υπάρχει πρακτορείο
efimeridhon edho konda?   εφημερίδων εδώ κοντά;

Do you sell ...?   *mipos poulate ...?*   Μήπως πουλάτε ...;
  English language   *anglofonez*   αγγλόφωνες
    newspapers   *efimeridhez*   εφημερίδες
  English language   *anglofona*   αγγλόφωνα
    magazines   *periodhika*   περιοδικά
  English language   *anglofona vivlia*   αγγλόφωνα
    books   βιβλία

Do you have any novels in
English?
  mipoz ehete mithistorimata   Μήπως έχετε μυθιστορήματα
  sta anglika?   στα αγγλικά;

I need ...	*hriazome ...*	Χρειάζομαι ...
airmail envelopes	*merikous aeroporikous fakellous*	μερικούς αεροπορικούς φακέλλους
an eraser	*ena zvistira*	ένα σβηστήρα
a highlighter	*mya markadhora*	μια μαρκαδόρα
glue	*kolla*	κόλλα
a pen	*ena stilo*	ένα στυλό
a pencil	*ena molivi*	ένα μολύβι
string	*spango*	σπάγγο
writing paper	*harti alliloghrafias*	χαρτί αλληλογραφίας

Thanks for your help.
efharisto ya ti voithia sas   Ευχαριστώ για τη βοήθειά σας.

Photography

Greece is an ideal place for photography and film of all kinds is widely available, though it tends to be on the expensive side. Good one-hour developing and printing services can be had in most Greek towns, if you are impatient to see the results of your efforts with your new dutyfree camera.

Do you sell film?
mipoz poulate film?   Μήπως πουλάτε φιλμ;

I'd like film with ...	*mou dhinete ena film me ...*	Μου δίνετε ένα φιλμ με ...
12 exposures	*dhodheka stasis*	δώδεκα στάσεις
24 exposures	*ikosi tesseriz stasis*	Είκοσι τέσσερεις στάσεις
36 exposures	*trianda exi stasis*	τριάντα έξη στάσεις

I'd like film for …	*mou dhinete ena film ya …*	Μου δίνετε ένα φιλμ για …
colour prints	*enhromez fotoghrafiez*	έγχρωμες φωτογραφίες
colour slides	*enhromez dhiafaniez*	έγχρωμες διαφάνειες
B&W photos	*aspromavrez fotoghrafiez*	ασπρόμαυρες φωτογραφίες

Can you develop this film?
borite na emfanisete afto to film?
Μπορείτε να εμφανίσετε αυτό το φιλμ;

When will the photos be ready?
pote tha ine etimez i fotoghrafiez?
Πότε θα είναι έτοιμες οι φωτογραφίες;

Can you develop slides?
borite na emfanisete dhiafaniez?
Μπορείτε να εμφανίσετε διαφάνειες;

Can I have two of each?
mou dhinete apo dhio?
Μου δίνετε από δυο;

I would like some reprints.
tha ithela merikez anatiposis
Θα ήθελα μερικές ανατυπώσεις.

My camera is broken.
halase i fotografiki mou mihani
Χάλασε η φωτογραφική μου μηχανή.

Can you repair it?
borite na ti ftiaxete?
Μπορείτε να τη φτιάξετε;

Do you sell video-8 cassette tapes?
mipoz poulate videokassetes ohto hilioston?
Μήπως πουλάτε βιντεοκασσέτες οχτώ χιλιοστών;

SHOPPING

I need some alkaline batteries.
hriazome merikez alkalikez   Χρειάζομαι μερικές αλκαλικές
batariez   μπαταρίες.

Some Useful Words

camera case	*thiki*	θήκη
filter	*filtro*	φίλτρο
flash	*flas*	φλας
light meter	*fotometro*	φωτόμετρο
telephoto lens	*tilefakos*	τηλεφακός
tripod	*tripodhas*	τρίποδας
wide-angle lens	*evrighonios fakos*	ευρυγώνιος φακός

Smoking

Greeks and Cypriots hold first place in Europe for smoking. Greece is not a place for nonsmokers – you have been warned! Though most people respect no-smoking areas to some degree, bus drivers quite often blithely ignore the rule and the public service is definitely one area where smoking is the rule rather than the exception. Smokers can fuel their habit at kiosks, and will certainly feel less social pressure than they might back home.

ΑΠΑΓΟΡΕΥΕΤΑΙ ΤΟ ΚΑΠΝΙΣΜΑ   NO SMOKING

A packet of …
ena paketo …   Ενα πακέτο …
Do you sell tobacco?
poulate kapno?   Πουλάτε καπνό;
A box of matches please.
ena kouti spirta, parakalo   Ενα κουτί σπίρτα παρακαλώ.

Do you sell lighters?
poulate anaptirez?

Πουλάτε αναπτήρες;

Could I have one of yours?
*boro na paro ena apo ta
dhika sas?*

Μπορώ να πάρω ένα από τα
δικά σας;

I am trying to give it up.
prospatho na to paratiso

Προσπαθώ να το παρατήσω.

It's a filthy habit, I know …
*to xero pos ine vromikh
sinithia …*

Το ξέρω πως είναι βρώμικη
συνήθεια …

Some Useful Words

cigarette	*tsigharo*	τσιγάρο
cigar	*pouro*	πούρο
nicotine	*nikotini*	νικοτίνη
pipe	*pipa*	πίπα
filter cigarettes	*tsighara me filtra*	τσιγάρα με φίλτρα
non-filter cigarettes	*tsighara horis filtra*	τσιγάρα χωρίς φίλτρα

Colours

With a clarity of light such as you will find in Greece, colours take on a new meaning. Here are the main ones. Remember: colours are adjectives and as such most of them change their endings depending on the gender and case of the word they are describing. Here we give you the masculine, feminine and neuter forms, where required.

beige	*bez*	μπεζ
black	*mavr-os/i/o*	μαύρ-ος/η/ο
blue	*ble*	μπλε
brown	*kaf-es/etia/i*	καφ-ές/ετιά/ετί
cyan	*kian-os/i/o*	κυαν-ός/ή/ό
gold	*hris-os/i/o*	χρυσ-ός/ή/ό
green	*prasin-os/i/o*	πράσιν-ος/η/ο
grey	*ghriz-os/a/o*	γκρίζ-ος/α/ο
indigo	*loulak-is/ia/i*	λουλακ-ής/ιά/ί
orange	*portokal-is/ia/i*	πορτοκαλ-ής/ιά/ί
pink	*roz*	ροζ
purple	*mov*	μοβ
red	*kokkin-os/i/o*	κόκκιν-ος/η/ο
silver	*asimeni-os/a/o*	ασημένι-ος/ια/ο
violet	*menexedh-is/ia/i*	μενεξεδ-ής/ιά/ί
white	*aspr-os/i/o*	άσπρ-ος/η/ο
yellow	*kitrin-os/i/o*	κίτριν-ος/η/ο
... dark	*... skour-os/a/o*	... σκούρ-ος/α/ο
... light	*... aniht-os/i/o*	... ανοιχτ-ός/ή/ό

Weights & Measures

The metric system is standard in Greece, but land measurement is usually referred to in 'stremmata' and occasionally weights will be referred to in the old traditional system.

SHOPPING

metre/s	*metro/a*	μέτρο/α
centimetre/s	*ekatosto/a*	εκατοστό/ά
millimetre/s	*xiliosto/a*	χιλιοστό/ά
litre/s	*litro/a*	λίτρο/α
kilogram/s	*kilo/a*	κιλό/ά
gram/s	*ghrammario/a*	γραμμάριο/α

Greek Measurements

'forearm' (64 cm)	*pihi*	πήχη
stremma (1,000 m²)	*stremma*	στρέμμα
oka (1,280 grams)	*oka*	οκά

Sizes & Comparisons

Standard 'continental' sizes for Europe are the rule here. Visitors from most English-speaking countries will have to adjust to the system.

Could I have a pair of size ... shoes?
  thelo ena zevghari Θέλω ένα ζευγάρι
  papoutsia noumero ...? παπούτσια νούμερο ...;
My size is ...
  to noumero mou ine ... Το νούμερό μου είναι ...
I take size ... in (Australia).
  stin (afstralia) perno Στην (Αυστραλία) παίρνω
  noumero ... νούμερο ...
Can I try them on?
  boro na ta dhokimaso? Μπορώ να τα δοκιμάσω;
They are too tight.
  mou erhonde poli sfihta Μου έρχονται πολύ σφιχτά.
Can I try another size?
  boro na dokimaso allo Μπορώ να δοκιμάσω άλλο
  noumero? νούμερο;

They don't fit.
  dhe mou horane   Δε μου χωράνε.
I'd like to try on a jacket.
  tha ithela na dhokimaso   Θα ήθελα να δοκιμάσω
  ena sakkaki   ένα σακκάκι.
It doesn't fit.
  dhe mou horaee   Δε μου χωράει.
It fits perfectly.
  mou horaee telia   Μου χωράει τέλεια.
It's too tight.
  mou erhete sfihto   Μου έρχεται σφιχτό.
It's too loose.
  mou erhete halaro   Μου έρχεται χαλαρό.
Can you alter it?
  borite na to mazepsete?   Μπορείτε να το μαζέψετε;
Can you measure me?
  borite na parete ta metra   Μπορείτε να πάρετε τα μέτρα
  mou?   μου;
I must lose some weight!
  prepi na haso varos!   Πρέπει να χάσω βάρος!
I am on a diet ...
  kano dhieta ...   Κάνω δίαιτα ...

SHOPPING

Health

Health care in Greece in generally good and reliable, but varies from location to location. There is a large number of doctors per head of population, so you should never be far from medical help whenever necessary. Many doctors will have trained abroad, or will have studied another language as part of their training, so you should not have too many problems in communicating. Still, there is nothing quite like being prepared for any eventuality. So, here is a compact linguistic first aid kit for your basic needs.

I need a doctor.
   hriazome yatro   Χρειάζομαι γιατρό.
It is an emergency!
   ine epighon!   Είναι επείγον!
I've injured myself.
   htipisa   Χτύπησα.
I am feeling sick.
   esthanome arostos   Αισθάνομαι άρρωστος.
Can you take me to a hospital?
   borite na me pate sto   Μπορείτε να με πάτε στο
   nosokomio?   νοσοκομείο;

General Complaints

I'm suffering from …	*pascho apo …*	Πάσχω από …
an earache	*pono sto afti*	πόνο στο αυτί
food poisoning	*trofiki dhilitiriasi*	τροφική δηλητηρίαση
a headache	*ponokefalo*	πονοκέφαλο

149

a sore throat	*pono sto lemo*	πόνο στο λαιμό
a stomachache	*pono sto stomahi*	πόνο στο στομάχι
sunburn	*iliokama*	ηλιόκαμα

I have sprained my ankle.
   eho stramboulixi ton astraghalo   Εχω στραμπουλήξει τον αστράγαλο.

I have burned myself.
   kaeeka   Κάηκα.

I have swallowed something.
   eho katapyee kati   Εχω καταπιεί κάτι.

I have a pain here.
   ponao edho   Πονάω εδώ.

I feel numb here.
   esthanome moudhiazma edho   Αισθάνομαι μούδιασμα εδώ.

I can't see properly.
   dhe vlepo kala   Δε βλέπω καλά.

Ailments

AIDS	*aydz*	EITZ
allergy	*alerghia*	αλλεργία
appendicitis	*skolikoeedhitidha*	σκωληκοειδίτιδα
arthritis	*arthritidha*	αρθρίτιδα
asthma	*asthma*	άσθμα
burn	*engavma*	έγκαυμα
cold	*kriologhima*	κρυολόγημα
constipation	*dhiskiliotita*	δυσκοιλιότητα
cough	*vihas*	βήχας
cramps	*kramba*	κράμπα
diabetes	*dhiavitis*	διαβήτης
diarrhoea	*dhiaria*	διάρροια
epilepsy	*epilipsia*	επιληψία
a fever	*piretos*	πυρετός
gout	*podhaghra*	ποδάγρα
hepatitis	*ipatitidha*	ηπατίτιδα
hiccups	*loxingas*	λόξυγγας
high blood pressure	*psili artiriaki piesi*	ψηλή αρτηριακή πίεση
indigestion	*dhispepsia*	δυσπεψία
an infection	*molinsi*	μόλυνση
influenza	*ghripi*	γρίππη
insomnia	*aeepnia*	αϋπνία
an itch	*faghoura*	φαγούρα
lice	*psirez*	ψείρες
low blood pressure	*hamili artiriaki piesi*	χαμηλή αρτηριακή πίεση
malaria	*elonosia*	ελονοσία
measles	*ilara*	ιλαρά
migraine	*imikrania*	ημικρανία
myopia	*miopia*	μυωπία

mumps	*parotitidha*	παρωτίτιδα
rabies	*lissa*	λύσσα
rheumatism	*revmatizmos*	ρευματισμός
swelling	*priximo*	πρήξιμο
tenosynovitis (RSI)	*tenondothikitidha*	τενοντοθηκίτιδα
tonsillitis	*amighdhalitidha*	αμυγδαλίτιδα
venereal disease	*afrodhisio nosima*	αφροδίσιο νόσημα
whooping cough	*kokitis*	κοκκύτης

Parts of the Body

ankle	*astraghalos*	αστράγαλος
appendix	*skolikoidhis*	σκωληκοειδής
	ipofisi	υπόφυση
arm	*heri/bratso*	χέρι/μπράτσο
bone	*kokalo*	κόκκαλο
ear	*afti*	αυτί
eye	*mati*	μάτι
foot	*podhi*	πόδι
hand	*heri*	χέρι
head	*kefali*	κεφάλι
heart	*kardhya*	καρδιά
kidney	*nefro*	νεφρό
leg	*podhi*	πόδι
liver	*sikoti*	σηκώτι
mouth	*stoma*	στόμα
muscle	*mis*	μυς
nose	*miti*	μύτη
teeth	*dhontia*	δόντια
throat	*lemos*	λαιμός
tongue	*ghlossa*	γλώσσα
ribs	*plevra*	πλευρά
stomach	*stomahi*	στομάχι
tendon	*tenondas*	τένοντας

At the Chemist

Do you have something
for …?
   mipoz ehete kati ya …?   Μήπως έχετε κάτι για … ;
Can you make up this
prescription?
   borite na mou ftiaxete   Μπορείτε να μου φτιάξετε
   afti ti sindaghi?   αυτή τη συνταγή;
When will it be ready?
   pote tha ine etimo?   Πότε θα είναι έτοιμο;
How many times a day?
   posez forez tin imera?   Πόσες φορές την ημέρα;
What do you advise?
   ti sinistate?   Τι συνιστάτε;

bandage	epidhezmos	επίδεσμος
aspirin	aspirini	ασπιρίνη
Band-aids	lefkoplast	λευκοπλάστ
comb	htena	χτένα
condoms	profilaktika	προφυλακτικά
	(kapotez)	(καπότες)
contraceptives	andisiliptika	αντισυλληπτικά
cough mixture	farmako ya viha	φάρμακο για βήχα
deodorant	aposmitiko	αποσμητικό
disinfectant	apolimandiko	απολυμαντικό
hairbrush	htena mallion	χτένα μαλλιών
lozenges	pastilyez	παστίλιες
moisturising cream	krema ghalaktos	κρέμα γάλακτος
needle	velona	βελόνα
razor	xirafi	ξυράφι
sanitary napkins	servietez	σερβιέττες
shampoo	sambouan	σαμπουάν
shaving cream	krema xirizmatos	κρέμα ξυρίσματος

HEALTH

soap	*sapouni*	σαπούνι
talcum powder	*poudhra*	πούδρα
tampons	*tambon*	ταμπόν
tissues	*hartomandila*	χαρτομάντηλα
toilet paper	*harti iyias*	χαρτί υγείας
toothbrush	*odhondovourtsa*	οδοντόβουρτσα
toothpaste	*odhondokrema*	οδοντόκρεμα

At the Dentist

There are plenty of good dentists in Greece. Although it's hard enough to strike up a conversation in the dentist's chair – never mind in Greek – the following expressions should see you through the tricky bits.

I need to see a dentist.
  prepi na pao ston   Πρέπει να πάω στον
  odhondiatro   οδοντίατρο.
I have a toothache.
  mou ponaee to dhondi   Μου πονάει το δόντι.
My gums are sore.
  mou ponane ta oula   Μου πονάνε τα ούλα.
I have an abcess.
  eho apostima tou dhondiou   Εχω απόστημα του δοντιού.
I think I need a filling.
  nomizo pos hriazome   Νομίζω πως χρειάζομαι
  sfraghizma   σφράγισμα.
Please don't take my tooth out!
  sas parakalo, mi mou   Σας παρακαλώ, μη μου
  vghalete to dhondi!   βγάλετε το δόντι!
Can you give me a local
anaesthetic?
  borite na mou kanete   Μπορείτε να μου κάνετε
  topiki anesthisia?   τοπική αναισθησία;

HEALTH

That hurts!
  ponaee! Πονάει!
Could I have a receipt?
  mou dhinete, parakalo Μου δίνετε, παρακαλώ,
  mya ghrapti apodhixi? μια γραπτή απόδειξη;

cleaning	*katharizma*	καθάρισμα
crown	*stefani*	στεφάνη
dentures	*masela*	μασέλα
extraction	*exaghoghi*	εξαγωγή
injection	*enesi*	ένεση
wisdom tooth	*fronimitis*	φρονιμίτης

Some Useful Words & Phrases

accident	*atihima*	ατύχημα
addiction (drug)	*narkomania*	ναρκομανία
antibiotics	*andiviotika*	αντιβιωτικά
antiseptic	*andisiptiko*	αντισηπτικό
bleeding	*emoraghia*	αιμορραγία
blood pressure	*artiriaki piesi*	αρτηριακή πίεση
blood test	*exetasi ematos*	εξέταση αίματος
contact lenses	*faki epafis*	φακοί επαφής
drugs (narcotics)	*narkotika*	ναρκωτικά
glasses	*yalya*	γυαλιά
medical insurance	*yatriki asfalya*	ιατρική ασφάλεια
medication	*farmako*	φάρμακο
menstruation	*periodhos*	περίοδος
ointment	*alifi*	αλοιφή
pills	*hapia*	χάπια
pregnancy	*engimosini*	εγκυμοσύνη
pregnant	*engios*	έγκυος
prescription	*sindayi*	συνταγή
sunglasses	*yalya iliou*	γυαλιά ηλίου

HEALTH

tablets	*hapia*	χάπια
vitamins	*vitaminez*	βιταμίνες
wound	*travma*	τραύμα

And at the end of the day, you can say …

I feel much better now!
   esthanome poli pyo   Αισθάνομαι πολύ πιο
   kala tora!   καλά τώρα!

Time, Dates & Holidays

Telling the Time

There are no special difficulties in telling the time in Greek, other than the fact that the Greek – like many people in warm climates – may have a different approach to time than you. But that's another story... If you have learned the numbers (see the next chapter) and the way to structure your sentence, based on the examples below, you are well on your way to mastering this aspect of your Greek Odyssey.

What time is it, please?
   ti ora ine, parakalo?   Τι ώρα είναι, παρακαλώ;

It is ...	*ine* ...	Είναι ...
1 o'clock	*mia i ora*	μια η ώρα
2 o'clock	*dhio i ora*	δύο η ώρα
6 o'clock	***exi** i ora*	έξη η ώρα
7.30	*efta ke misi*	εφτά και μισή
10.30	*dheka ke misi*	δέκα και μισή
4.15	*teseris ke tetarto*	τέσσερεις και τέταρτο
11.15	***endheka** ke tetarto*	ένδεκα και τέταρτο
7.45	*ohto **para** tetarto*	οχτώ πάρα τέταρτο
11.45	*dhodeka **para** tetarto*	δώδεκα πάρα τέταρτο
4.10	*teseris ke dheka*	τέσσερεις και δέκα
2.40	*tris **para** ikosi*	τρεις πάρα είκοσι

in the morning	*to proi*	το πρωί
in the afternoon	*to mesimeri*	το μεσημέρι
in the evening	*to bradhi*	το βράδυ
at night	*ti nihta*	τη νύχτα

Days of the Week

No real surprises here. It might be worth mentioning that days Monday to Thursday are based on the ordinal numerals, Monday being the second day of the week, and so on until Friday, which is the day of 'preparation'. Saturday is the 'Sabbath' and Sunday the 'Day of the Lord'. Here they are:

Sunday	*kiriaki*	Κυριακή
Monday	*deftera*	Δευτέρα
Tuesday	*triti*	Τρίτη
Wednesday	*tetarti*	Τετάρτη
Thursday	*pempti*	Πέμπτη
Friday	*paraskevi*	Παρασκευή
Saturday	*savato*	Σάββατο

Months

Yes, there are only 12 of them in Greece too. They are very similar to their English counterparts, so should not be too hard to remember.

January	*yanouarios*	Ιανουάριος
February	*fevrouarios*	Φεβρουάριος
March	*martios*	Μάρτιος
April	*aprilios*	Απρίλιος
May	*mayios*	Μάιος
June	*younios*	Ιούνιος

July	*youlios*	Ιούλιος
August	*avghoustos*	Αύγουστος
September	*septemvrios*	Σεπτέμβριος
October	*octovrios*	Οκτώβριος
November	*noemvrios*	Νοέμβριος
December	*dekemvrios*	Δεκέμβριος

Seasons

summer	*kalokeri*	Καλοκαίρι
autumn/fall	*fthinoporo*	Φθινόπωρο
winter	*himonas*	Χειμώνας
spring	*aniksi*	Άνοιξη

Dates

Forming dates in Greek is fairly logical, but you do need to know
the cardinal and ordinal numbers. The ordinal number of the date
refers to the word 'day' (ημέρα) so the ordinal is a feminine adjective. When saying 'on' a particular day, we do not use a word
for 'on' in Greek. Rather, we say the day as if it was the object of
the sentence e.g. on Tuesday, *tin triti,* την Τρίτη. For dates we
usually use στις (*stis*). Here are some illustrative examples.

Today is Monday.
    simera ine deftera   Σήμερα είναι Δευτέρα.
I shall leave on Wednesday.
    tha figho tin detarti   Θα φύγω την Τετάρτη.
I arrive on the 7th of August.
    ftano stis efta avgoustou   Φτάνω στις εφτά Αυγούστου.
What is the date today?
    pya imerominia ehoume   Ποια ημερομηνία έχουμε
    simera?   σήμερα;
It is the 1st of April, 1995.
    ine proti apriliou tou   Είναι πρώτη Απριλίου του
    hilia enyakosia eneninda   χίλια εννεακόσια ενενήντα
    pende   πέντε.
We go to Greece in the
summer.
    piyenoume stin elladha   Πηγαίνουμε στην Ελλάδα
    to kalokeri   το καλοκαίρι.

Present

today	*simera*	σήμερα
now	*tora*	τώρα
this morning	*to proi*	το πρωί
this afternoon	*to apoyevma*	το απόγευμα
this evening	*apopse*	απόψε
this week	*afti tin evdhomadha*	αυτή την εβδομάδα
this month	*afto to mina*	αυτό το μήνα
this year	*fetos*	Φέτος

Past

yesterday	*hthez*	χθες
then	*tote*	τότε
the day before yesterday	*prohthez*	προχθές
last Saturday	*to perazmeno savato*	το περασμένο Σάββατο
last week	*tim berazmeni evdhomadha*	την περασμένη εβδομάδα
last month	*tom berazmeno mina*	τον περασμένο μήνα
last year	*perisi*	πέρυσι

Future

tomorrow	*avrio*	αύριο
the day after tomorrow	*methavrio*	μεθαύριο
tomorrow morning	*avrio to proi*	αύριο το πρωί
next Sunday	*tin alli kiriaki*	την άλλη Κυριακή
next week	*tin alli evdhomadha*	την άλλη εβδομάδα
next month	*ton allo mina*	τον άλλο μήνα
next year	*tou hronou*	του χρόνου

Some Useful Words

a year ago	*edho ke ena hrono*	εδώ και ένα χρόνο
always	*panda*	πάντα
at this moment	*afti ti stighmi*	αυτή τη στιγμή
century	*eonas*	αιώνας
during …	*kata ti dhiarkia …*	κατά τη διάρκεια …
early	*noris*	νωρίς
every day	*kathe mera*	κάθε μέρα
for the time being	*ya tin ora*	για την ώρα
for ever	*ya panda*	για πάντα
just now	*molis tora*	μόλις τώρα
late	*argha*	αργά
later on	*pyo argha*	πιο αργά
never	*pote*	ποτέ
not any more	*pote pya*	ποτέ πια
not yet	*ohi akoma*	όχι ακόμα
since then	*apo tote*	από τότε
sometimes	*merikez forez*	μερικές φορές
sundown	*iliovasilema*	ηλιοβασίλεμα
sunrise	*harama*	χάραμα
soon	*sindoma*	σύντομα
still	*akoma*	ακόμα
straight away	*amesos*	αμέσως

National Holidays

Like most countries anywhere, Greece has a good sprinkling of national and local holidays and feast days – especially saints' days. Here are some of the major ones that you may encounter.

One ubiquitous expression that seems to suffice for most festive occasions is:

(lit) Many years!	*hronia polla!*	Χρόνια πολλά!

New Year's Day (1 January) Πρωτοχρονιά *(protohronya)*. As in many Western countries, 1 January is the beginning of the new year and is celebrated in Greece in much the same way. Playing cards is a traditional way to spend New Year's Eve. People exchange the greeting Καλή Χρονιά *(kali hronya)* when the New Year has arrived.

25th of March (25 March) Εικοστή Πέμπτη Μαρτίου *(ikosti pempti martiou)*. Greece's National Day, celebrating the anniversary of their freedom from the Turkish yoke in 1821. A day of parades, pomp and ceremony.

Easter (date varies) Πάσχα *(pascha)*. This is by far the most important feast in the Greek religious and national calendar. There are many greetings and customs that are related to this period of the year. See the Small Talk chapter, page 48, for these.

May Day (1 May) Πρωτομαγιά *(protomaya)*. Traditionally the first day of the summer season but also celebrated as workers' solidarity day.

'OHI' Day (28 October) Εικοστή Ογδόη Οκτωβρίου *(ikosti oghdoee oktovriou)*. Celebating the day Greeks said 'no' – όχι *(ohi)* to Mussolini's ultimatum to surrender, which ultimately led to the Dictator's ill-conceived invasion of Albania and attempt to invade Greece. More pomp and ceremony.

(The Heroes of the) Polytechnic (17 November) 'Το Πολυτεχνείο' *(to polytehnio)*. In honour of the fallen students who were killed by the tanks of the Junta Generals in November, 1974, while occupying the Athens Polytechnic during a general student protest against the military régime.

Christmas (25 December) Χριστούγεννα *(hristouyenna)*. Celebrated like elsewhere in the Christian world, with Christmas trees, decorations and present giving. Children go from house to house singing traditional Christmas carols.

Be aware of local feast days – particularly those honouring saints – when shops, businesses and services may be unexpectedly closed.

Numbers & Amounts

Cardinal Numbers

Greek numbering presents few difficulties once you have mastered the basic numerical roots. Some Greek numbers (typically those containing one, three and four) are like adjectives and correspond according to the gender of the noun they qualify. Other than some occasional spelling differences, there is not much to do other than learn the numbers by heart. Remember that many Greek numbers appear in scientific names in English: e.g. pentagram (a five-cornered star); hexagon (a six-sided shape); decade (10 years), so you have half the work already done for you.

1	*enas/mia/ena*	ένας/μια/ένα (m/f/n)
2	*dhio*	δύο
3	*tris*	τρεις (m & f)
	tria	τρία (n)
4	*teseris*	τέσσερεις (m & f)
	tesera	τέσσερα (n)
5	*pende*	πέντε
6	*exi*	έξη
7	*efta*	εφτά
8	*ohto*	οχτώ
9	*enea*	εννέα
10	*dheka*	δέκα
11	*endheka*	ένδεκα
12	*dhodheka*	δώδεκα
13	*dheka-tris*	δεκατρείς (m & f)
	dheka-tria	δεκατρία (n)

14	*dheka-teseris*	δεκατέσσερεις (m & f)
	dheka-tesera	δεκατέσσερα (n)
15	*dheka-pende*	δεκαπέντε
16	*dheka-exi*	δεκαέξη
17	*dheka-efta*	δεκαεφτά
18	*dheka-ohto*	δεκαοχτώ
19	*dheka-enea*	δεκαεννέα
20	*ikosi*	είκοσι
21	*ikosi-ena*	εικοσιένα (m & n)
	ikosi-mia	εικοσιμία (f)
30	*trianda*	τριάντα
40	*saranda*	σαράντα
50	*peninda*	πενήντα
60	*exinda*	εξήντα
70	*evdhominda*	εβδομήντα
80	*oghdhonda*	ογδόντα
90	*eneninda*	ενενήντα
100	*ekato(n)*	εκατό

NUMBERS

129	*ekaton ikosi enea*	εκατόν είκοσι εννέα
200	*dhiakosi-i/ez/a*	δυακόσι-οι/ες/α
300	*triakosi-i/ez/a*	τριακόσι-οι/ες/α
400	*tetrakosi-i/ez/a*	τετρακόσι-οι/ες/α
500	*pendakosi-i/ez/a*	πεντακόσι-οι/ες/α
600	*exakosi-i/ez/a*	εξακόσι-οι/ες/α
700	*eftakosi-i/ez/a*	εφτακόσι-οι/ες/α
800	*ohtakosi-i/ez/a*	οχτακόσι-οι/ες/α
900	*enyakosi-i/ez/a*	εννιακόσι-οι/ες/α
1000	*hili-i/ez/a*	χίλι-οι/ες/α
2000	*dhio hiliadhez*	δυο χιλιάδες
one million	*ena ekatomirio*	ένα εκατομμύριο
two million	*dhio ekatomiria*	δυο εκατομμύρια

Ordinal Numbers

Ordinal numbers in Greek all behave like adjectives, so you need to know the gender of the noun you wish to qualify with an ordinal number beforehand. The system is logical, though it does tend to get a bit complicated when long numbers are involved. Given here are the masculine, feminine and neuter forms of the ordinals.

1st	*prot-os/i/o*	πρώτ-ος/η/ο
2nd	*defter-os/i/o*	δεύτερ-ος/η/ο
3rd	*tritos/i/o*	τρίτ-ος/η/ο
4th	*tetart-os/i/o*	τέταρτ-ος/η/ο
5th	*pempt-os/i/o*	πέμπτ-ος/η/ο
6th	*ekt-os/i/o*	έκτ-ος/η/ο
7th	*evdhom-os/i/o*	έβδομ-ος/η/ο
8th	*oghdo-os/i/o*	όγδο-ος/η/ο
9th	*enat-os/i/o*	ένατ-ος/η/ο
10th	*dhekat-os/i/o*	δέκατ-ος/η/ο

Fractions

Unless you are going to be particular meticulous about your numbers, you probably won't have much use for fractions, but here are the main ones anyway.

one-half	miso	μισό
one-quarter	tetarto	τέταρτο
one-third	trito	τρίτο
two-thirds	dhio trita	δύο τρίτα
three-quarters	tria tetarta	τρία τέταρτα

Some Useful Phrases

You are most likely to use numbers when shopping, changing money, or maybe even discussing the latest football score with Greeks! Many expressions with numbers are in the other chapters; but here are one or two more that might see you through any conversation.

Half a kilo of … please.
 miso kilo … parakalo Μισό κιλό … παρακαλώ.
Five hundred drachmas worth
of … please.
 ena penadakosiariko … Ενα πεντακοσιάρικο …
 parakalo παρακαλώ.
Forty litres of super (petrol).
 saranda litra souper Σαράντα λίτρα σούπερ.
Two hundred and fifty grams
of Kalamata olives.
 dhiakosia gramaria elies Διακόσια γραμμάρια ελιές
 kalamatas, parakalo Καλαμάτας, παρακαλώ.
I am … years old.
 ime … hronon Είμαι … χρονών.

I was only doing 100 km an hour!
> *etreha mono me ekato hiliometra tin ora!*

Ετρεχα μόνο με εκατό χιλιόμετρα την ώρα!

Vocabulary

A

able, to be (can)	boro	μπορώ
Can I take a	boro na vghalo	Μπορώ να βγάλω
photograph?	mya fotografia?	μια φωτογραφία;
above	epano	επάνω
abroad	exoteriko	εξωτερικό
accept, I	dhehome	δέχομαι
accept, you	dhehese	δέχεσαι
accident	atyhima	ατύχημα
accommodation	steghasi	στέγαση
addict (drug)	narkomanis	ναρκομανής
addiction (drug)	narkomania	ναρκομανία
address	dhiefthynsi	διεύθυνση
administration	dhiikisi	διοίκηση
admission	omologhia	ομολογία
adventure	peripetya	περιπέτεια
advice	symvouli	συμβουλή
advise	symvoulevo	συμβουλεύω
after	meta	μετά
again	xana	ξανά
against	enandi	έναντι
age	ilikia	ηλικία
agree, I	symfono	συμφωνώ
agree, you	symfonis	συμφωνείς
agriculture	gheorgia	γεωργία
ahead	brosta	μπροστά
aid	voithya	βοήθεια

air-conditioned	*klimatozomen-os/i/o*	κλιματιζόμεν-ος/η/ο
airline	*aeroporia*	αεροπορία
airmail	*aeroporikos*	αεροπορικώς
all	*ol-os/i/o*	όλ-ος/η/ο
allow	*epitrepo*	επιτρέπω
almost	*shedhon*	σχεδόν
alone	*mon-os/i/o*	μόν-ος/η/ο
also	*episis*	επίσης
alternative	*enallaktik-os/i/o*	εναλλακτικ-ός/ή/ό
always	*panda*	πάντα
amazing	*katapliktik-os/i/o*	καταπληκτικ-ός/ή/ό
ambassador	*prezvys*	πρέσβυς
among	*anamesa*	ανάμεσα
ancient	*arhe-os/a/o*	αρχαί-ος/α/ο

VOCABULARY

and	*ke*	και
angry	*thymomen-os/i/o*	θυμωμέν-ος/η/ο
answer (n)	*apandisi*	απάντηση
answer (v)	*apando*	απαντώ
antique	*andika*	αντίκα
anytime	*opotedhipote*	οποτεδήποτε
appointment	*randevou*	ραντεβού
approximately	*kata prosengisi*	κατά προσέγγιση
archaeological	*arheoloyik-os/i/o*	αρχαιολογικ-ός/ή/ό
argue	*filoniko*	φιλονικώ
argument	*filonikia*	φιλονικία
arrive	*ftano*	φτάνω
art	*tehni*	τέχνη
ask	*roto*	ρωτώ
ashtray	*stahtothiki*	σταχτοθήκη
asleep	*kimizmen-os/i/o*	κοιμισμέν-ος/η/ο
at	*sto/sti*	στο/στη
automatic	*aftomat-os/i/o*	αυτόματ-ος/η/ο

B

baby	*moro*	μωρό
babysitter	*babysitter*	μπεϊμπισίττερ
backpack	*sakkidhyo*	σακκίδιο
bad	*kak-os/i/o*	κακ-ός/ή/ό
bag	*tsanda*	τσάντα
baggage	*apsokevez*	αποσκευές
ball	*bala*	μπάλα
bank	*trapeza*	τράπεζα
bar	*bar*	μπαρ
barbeque	*psistarya*	ψησταριά
battery	*bataria*	μπαταρία

beach	*paralia*	παραλία
beautiful	*ore-os/a/o/*	ωραί-ος/α/ο
because	*dhioti*	διότι
bed	*krevati*	κρεββάτι
bedbugs	*koryi*	κοριοί
before	*prin*	πριν
beggar	*zitianos*	ζητιάνος
beginner	*arharios*	αρχάριος
behind	*piso*	πίσω
below	*apo kato*	από κάτω
beside	*dhipla*	δίπλα
best	*o/i/to kalyter-os/i/o*	οη/το καλύτερ-ος/ηþ
better	*kalyter-os/i/o*	καλύτερ-ος/η/ο
between	*metaksi*	μεταξύ
bicycle	*podhilato*	ποδήλατο
big	*meghal-os/i/o*	μεγάλ-ος/η/ο
bill (account)	*loghariazmos*	λογαριασμός
birthday	*yenethlia*	γεννέθλια
bitter	*pikr-os/i/o*	πικρ-ός/ή/ό
black	*mavr-os/i/o*	μαύρ-ος/η/ο
bless (v)	*evlogho*	ευλογώ
blind	*tyfl-os/i/o*	τυφλ-ός/ή/ό
boat	*varka*	βάρκα
bomb	*vomva*	βόμβα
book (n)	*vivlio*	βιβλίο
bookshop	*vivliopolio*	βιβλιοπωλείο
bored, I'm	*varyeme*	βαριέμαι
borrow	*dhanizome*	δανείζομαι
boss	*afendiko*	αφεντικό
both	*kai i/ta dhio*	και οι/τα δυο
bottle	*boukali*	μπουκάλι
bottle opener	*anihtiri*	ανοιχτήρι

box	*kouti*	κουτί
boy	*aghori*	αγόρι
boyfriend	*filos*	φίλος
brave	*tolmir-os/i/o*	τολμηρ-ός/ή/ο
break (v)	*spazo*	σπάζω
break, rest (n)	*dhialima*	διάλειμμα
breakfast	*proïno*	πρωινό
bribe (n)	*dhorodhokia*	δωροδοκία
bribe (v)	*dhorodhoko*	δωροδοκώ
bridge	*yefira*	γέφυρα
bright	*lambr-os/i/o*	λαμπρ-ός/ή/ό
bring	*ferno*	φέρνω
broken	*spazmen-os/i/o*	σπασμέν-ος/η/ο
building	*htirio*	χτίριο
burn (v)	*keo*	καίω
bus	*leoforio*	λεωφορείο
business	*epihirisi*	επιχείρηση
busy	*apasholimen-os/i/o*	απασχολημέν-ος/η/ο
but	*alla*	αλλά
buy	*aghorazo*	αγοράζω

C

café	*kafeteria*	καφετέρια
camera	*fotoghrafiki mihani*	φωτογραφική μηχανή
camp (v)	*kataskinono*	κατασκηνώνω
camp (n)	*kataskinosi*	κατασκήνωση
can opener	*anihtiri*	ανοιχτήρι
candle	*keri*	κερί
capitalism	*kapitalizmos*	καπιταλισμός
cards (playing)	*trapoula*	τράπουλα

care (to take care of)	*frondizo*	φροντίζω
careful	*prosehtik-os/i/o*	προσεχτικ-ός/ή/ό
carry	*kouvalo*	κουβαλώ
cashier	*tamio*	ταμείο
cemetery	*nekrotafio*	νεκροταφείο
certain	*sighour-os/i/o*	σίγουρ-ος/η/ο
chance	*efkeria*	ευκαιρία
chair	*karekla*	καρέκλα
change (coins)	*psila*	ψιλά
change (trains)	*allazo*	αλλάζω
cheap	*ftin-os/i/o*	φτην-ός/ή/ό
chemist (pharmacy)	*farmakio*	φαρμακείο
choose	*dhialegho*	διαλέγω
cigarettes	*tsighara*	τσιγάρα
cigarette papers	*harti tsigharon*	χαρτί τσιγάρων
city	*poli*	πόλη
city centre	*kendro*	κέντρο
clean	*kathar-os/i/o*	καθαρ-ός/ή/ό
close (adj)	*kondin-os/i/o*	κοντιν-ός/ή/ό
coat	*palto*	παλτό
cold	*kri-os/a/o*	κρύ-ος/α/ο
comfortable	*anet-os/i/o*	άνετ-ος/η/ο
communism	*kommounizmos*	κομμουνισμός
company	*eteria*	εταιρεία
complex (adj)	*periplok-os/i/o*	περίπλοκ-ος/η/ο
condom	*profylaktiko*	προφυλακτικό
Congratulations!	*sinharitiria*	Συγχαρητήρια!
contact lens	*fakos epafis*	φακός επαφής
contagious	*kollitik-os/i/o*	κολλητικ-ός/ή/ό
contraceptive	*andisyliptiko*	αντισυλληπτικό
conversation	*syzitisi*	συζήτηση
cook (v)	*mayirevo*	μαγειρεύω

corner	*ghonia*	γωνία
corruption	*diafthora*	διαφθορά
count (v)	*metro*	μετρώ
courtyard	*avli*	αυλή
crazy	*trell-os/i/o*	τρελλ-ός/ή/ό
credit card	*pistotiki karta*	πιστωτική κάρτα
crop	*sodhya*	σοδειά
customs (officials)	*teloniaki*	τελωνειακοί
cut (v)	*kovo*	κόβω

D

daily	*kathimerinos*	καθημεριν-ός/ή/ό
damp	*yghr-os/i/o*	υγρ-ός/ή/ό
dangerous	*epikindhyn-os/i/o*	επικίνδυν-ος/η/ο
dark	*skotin-os/i/o*	σκοτειν-ός/ή/ό
date (time)	*hmerominia*	ημερομηνία
dawn	*avyi*	αυγή
day	*mera*	μέρα
dead	*pethamen-os/i/o*	πεθαμέν-ος/η/ο
deaf	*kouf-os/i/o*	κουφ-ός/ή/ό
death	*thanatos*	θάνατος
decide	*apofasizo*	αποφασίζω
decision	*apofasi*	απόφαση
delicious	*nostim-os/i/o*	νόστιμ-ος/η/ο
delightful	*efharist-os/i/o*	ευχάριστ-ος/η/ο
democracy	*dhimokratia*	δημοκρατία
demonstration (protest)	*dhiadhilosi*	διαδήλωση
depart	*anahoro*	αναχωρώ
departure	*anahorisi*	αναχώρηση
desert	*erimos*	έρημος

VOCABULARY

destroy	*katastrefo*	καταστρέφω
development	*anaptixi*	ανάπτυξη
dictatorship	*dhiktatoria*	δικτατορία
dictionary	*lexiko*	λεξικό
different	*dhiaforetik-os/i/o*	διαφορετικ-ός/ή/ό
difficult	*dhyskol-os/i/o*	δύσκολ-ος/η/ο
dinner	*dhipno*	δείπνο
dirt	*vromya*	βρωμιά
dirty	*vromik-os/i/o*	βρώμικ-ος/η/ο
disadvantage	*mionektima*	μειονέκτημα
discount	*ekptosi*	έκπτωση
discrimination	*dhiakrisi*	διάκριση
disinfectant	*apolymandiko*	απολυμαντικό
distant	*makrin-os/i/o*	μακριν-ός/ή/ό
doctor	*yatros*	ιατρός
dole	*epidhoma anerghias*	επίδομα ανεργίας
doll	*koukla*	κούκλα
double	*dhipl-os/i/o*	διπλ-ός/ή/ό
down	*kato*	κάτω
downstairs	*apo kato*	από κάτω
downtown	*kendro*	κέντρο
dream (n)	*oniro*	όνειρο
dried	*xiramen-os/i/o*	ξηραμέν-ος/η/ο
drink (n)	*poto*	ποτό
drink (v)	*pino*	πίνω
drinkable (water)	*posimo (nero)*	πόσιμο (νερό)
drugs	*narkotika*	ναρκωτικά
drunk (inebriated)	*methyzmen-os/i/o*	μεθυσμέν-ος/η/ο
dry	*xir-os/i/o*	ξηρ-ός/ή/ό
during	*kata ti dhiarkia*	κατά τη διάρκεια
dust	*skoni*	σκόνη

E

each	*kathe*	κάθε
early	*noris*	νωρίς
earn	*kerdhizo*	κερδίζω
earnings	*isodhima*	εισόδημα
Earth	*yi*	Γη
earthquake	*sizmos*	σεισμός
easy	*efkol-os/i/o*	εύκολ-ος/η/ο
eat	*tro-o*	τρώω
economical	*ikonomik-os/i/o*	οικονομικ-ός/ή/ό
economy	*ikonomia*	οικονομία
education	*pedhia*	παιδεία
elections	*ekloyez*	εκλογές
electricity	*ilektrizmos*	ηλεκτρισμός
elevator (lift)	*asanser*	ασανσέρ
embassy	*prezvia*	πρεσβεία
employer	*erghodotis*	εργοδότης
empty	*adhy-os/a/o*	άδει-ος/α/ο
end	*telos*	τέλος
energy	*energhia*	ενέργεια
English	*anglika*	Αγγλικά
enjoy (oneself)	*dhiaskedhazo*	διασκεδάζω
enough	*arket-os/i/o*	αρκετ-ός/ή/ό
enter	*beno*	μπαίνω
entry	*isodhos*	είσοδος
equal	*is-os/i/o*	ίσ-ος/η/ο
evening	*vradhy*	βράδυ
event	*ekdhilosi*	εκδήλωση
every	*kathe*	κάθε
every day	*kathe mera*	κάθε μέρα
everyone	*olos o kozmos*	όλος ο κόσμος
everything	*ta panda*	τα πάντα

VOCABULARY

exchange (vb)	*andalasso*	ανταλλάσσω
exhausted	*exandlimen-os/i/o*	εξαντλημένος
exile	*exoria*	εξορία
expensive	*akriv-os/i/o*	ακριβ-ός/ή/ό
experience	*embiria, pira*	εμπειρία, πείρα
export (v)	*exagho*	εξάγω
export (n)	*exaghoghi*	εξαγωγή

F

false	*psevd-is/is/es*	ψευδ-ής/ής/ές
family	*ikoyenia*	οικογένεια
fan (cooling)	*anemistiras*	ανεμιστήρας
far	*makrin-os/i/o*	μακριν-ός/ή/ό
farm	*aghroktima*	αγρόκτημα
fast (not eating)	*nistevo*	νηστεύω
fast (quick)	*ghrighor-os/i/o*	γρήγορ-ος/η/ο
fat	*hondr-os/i/o*	χοντρ-ός/ή/ό
fault (technical)	*elattoma*	ελάττωμα
fault, my	*dhiko mou sfalma*	δικό μου σφάλμα
fear	*fovos*	φόβος
fee	*amivi*	αμοιβή
feel (v)	*esthanome*	αισθάνομαι
feeling	*esthisi*	αίσθηση
ferry	*ferrybot, porthmio*	φερρυμπότ, πορθμείο
festival	*yorti*	γιορτή
fever	*pyretos*	πυρετός
few	*ligh-os/i/o*	λίγ-ος/η/ο
fiancé/ée	*aravoniastik-os/ya*	αρραβωνιαστικ-ός/ιά
film (movie)	*(kinimatoghrafiko) ergho*	(κινηματογραφικό) έργο

VOCABULARY

film (roll of)	*film*	φιλμ
fine (penalty)	*prostimo*	πρόστιμο
fire	*fotya*	φωτιά
firewood	*kafsoxyla*	καυσόξυλα
flag	*simea*	σημαία
flashlight (torch)	*fakos*	φακός
flood	*plimyra*	πλημμύρα
floor	*patoma*	πάτωμα
follow	*akoloutho*	ακολουθώ
food	*fayito*	φαγητό
food poisoning	*trofiki dhilitiriash*	τροφική δηλητηρίαση
foreign	*allodhap-os/i/o*	αλλοδαπ-ός/ή/ό
forever	*ya panda*	για πάντα
forget (v)	*xehno*	ξεχνώ
I forgot.	*xehasa*	ξέχασα.
You forgot.	*xehases*	ξέχασες.
forgive	*sinhoro*	συγχωρώ
formal	*episim-os/i/o*	επίσημ-ος/η/ο
fragile	*evthrafst-os/i/o*	εύθραυστ-ος/η/ο
free (of charge)	*dhorean*	δωρεάν
free (not bound)	*elefther-os/i/o*	ελεύθερ-ος/η/ο

freeze	paghono	παγώνω
fresh (not stale)	fresk-os/i/o	φρέσκ-ος/η/ο
friend	filos, fili	φίλος (m), φίλη (f)
friendly	filik-os/i/o	φιλικ-ός/ή/ό
full	yemat-os/i/o	γεμάτ-ος/η/ο
fun	dhiaskedhasi	διασκέδαση
funny	asti-os/a/o	αστείος

G

game	pehnidhi	παιχνίδι
garbage	skoupidhya	σκουπίδια
garden	kipos	κήπος
gas	fotaerio	φωταέριο
gas cartridge/ cylinder	fiali fotaeriou	φιάλη φωταερίου
gate	pyli	πύλη
generous	yeneodhor-os/i/o/	γενναιόδωρ-ος/η/ο
girl	koritsi	κορίτσι
girlfriend	filenadha	φιλενάδα
give	dhino	δίνω
Give me ...	dhose mou ...	Δώσε μου ...
I'll give you ...	tha sou dhoso	Θα σου δώσω ...
glass (of water)	potiri (nero)	ποτήρι (νερό)
glasses	yalya	γυαλιά
go	piyeno	πηγαίνω
I'm going to ...	piyeno sto/sti ...	Πηγαίνω στο/στη...
God	theos	Θεός
good	kal-os/i/o	καλ-ός/ή/ό
government	kyvernisi	κυβέρνηση
greedy	lemargh-os/i/o	λαίμαργ-ος/η/ο
grow (v)	meghalono	μεγαλώνω

VOCABULARY

guess (v)	*mandevo*	μαντεύω
guide (n)	*xenaghos*	ξεναγός
guidebook	*touristikos odhighos*	τουριστικός οδηγός
guilty	*enoh-os/i/o*	ένοχος
guitar	*kithara*	κιθάρα

H

half	*mis-os/i/o*	μισ-ός/ή/ό
handbag	*tsanda*	τσάντα
handicrafts	*hirotehnia*	χειροτεχνία
handsome	*omorf-os/i/o*	όμορφ-ος/η/ο
happy	*haroumen-os/i/o*	χαρούμεν-ος/η/ο
hard	*sklir-os/i/o*	σκληρ-ός/ή/ό
hate (vb)	*miso*	μισώ
have	*eho*	έχω
I have ...	*(egho) eho*	(εγώ) έχω
you have ...	*(esis) ehete*	(εσείς) έχετε
Have you (got) ...?	*ehete ...?*	έχετε ...;
health	*iyia*	υγεία
hear	*akouo*	ακούω
heat	*zesta, thermansi*	ζέστα, θέρμανση
heater	*kalorifer*	καλοριφέρ
heavy	*var-ys/ya/y*	βαρ-ύς/ιά/ύ
Hello!	*ya sas!*	Γεια σας
help (v)	*voitho*	βοηθώ
here	*edho*	εδώ
high	*psil-os/i/o*	ψηλ-ός/ή/ό
hill	*lofos*	λόφος
hire	*nikyazo*	νοικιάζω
I'd like to hire it.	*thelo na to nikyaso*	θέλω να το νοικιάσω.

hitchhike	*otostop*	ωτοστόπ
holiday	*dhiakopez*	διακοπές
holy	*ayi-os/a/o*	άγι-ος/α/ο
home	*spiti*	σπίτι
homeland	*patridha*	πατρίδα
homosexual	*omofilofylos*	ομοφιλόφυλος
honest	*timi-os/a/o*	τίμι-ος/α/ο
hope (v)	*elpizo*	ελπίζω
hope (n)	*elpidha*	ελπίδα
hospitality	*filoxenia*	φιλοξενία
hot	*zest-os/i/o*	ζεστ-ός/ή/ό
hotel	*xenodhohio*	ξενοδοχείο
house	*spiti*	σπίτι
housework	*dhoulyez tou spitiou*	δουλειές του σπιτιού
how	*pos*	πώς
How do I get to ...?	*pos tha pao sto...?*	Πώς θα πάω στο...;
How much is ...?	*poso kani ...?*	Πόσο κάνει ...;
How are you?	*ti kanete?*	Τι κάνετε;
human	*anthropos*	άνθρωπος
I'm hungry.	*pinao*	Πεινάω.
Are you hungry?	*pinate*	Πεινάτε;
hurry, I'm in a	*viazome*	βιάζομαι
hurt	*plighono*	πληγώνω
hypnotism	*ypnotizmos*	υπνωτισμός

I

ice	*paghos*	πάγος
idea	*idhea*	ιδέα
identification	*taftotita*	ταυτότητα
if	*an*	αν

VOCABULARY

ill	**arr**ost-os/i/o	άρρωστ-ος/η/ο
illegal	pa**ranom**-os/i/o	παράνομ-ος/η/ο
imagination	fandasia	φαντασία
immediately	amesos	αμέσως
imitation	apomimisi	απομίμηση
import (v)	is**agho**	εισάγω
import (n)	isagho**ghi**	εισαγωγή
impossible	adhynat-os/i/o	αδύνατ-ος/η/ο
imprisonment	fy**laki**si	φυλάκιση
in	mesa	μέσα
included	symberilamva-nomen-os/i/o	συμπεριλαμβα-νόμεν-ος/η/ο
inconvenient	akatallil-os/i/o	ακατάλληλ-ος/η/ο
industry	viomihania	βιομηχανία
infection	molynsi	μόλυνση
infectious	molyndik-**os/i/o**	μολυντικ-ός/ή/ό
informal	anepisim-os/i/o	ανεπίσημ-ος/η/ο
information	pliroforiez	πληροφορίες
injection	enesi	ένεση
injury	htypima	χτύπημα
insect repellant	apothotiko endomon	αποθωτικό εντόμων
inside	mesa	μέσα
insurance	asfalya	ασφάλεια
insure (v)	asfalizo	ασφαλίζω
insured, It's	ine asfaliz-men-os/i/o	είναι ασφαλισ-μέν-ος/η/ο
intelligent	exypn-os/i/o	έξυπν-ος/η/ο
interested, I'm	endhiafe**rome**	ενδιαφέρομαι
interesting	endhiafer-on/-ousa/-on	ενδιαφέρ-ων/-ουσα/ον

| international | *dhiethn-is/is/es* | διεθν-ής/ής/ές |
| invite (v) | *proskalo* | προσκαλώ |

J

jail	*fylaki*	φυλακή
jazz	*tzaz*	τζαζ
jeans	*blou-tzin*	μπλου-τζήν
jewellery	*kozmimata*	κοσμήματα
job	*dhoulya*	δουλειά
joke (n)	*astio*	αστείο
I'm joking.	*astievome*	Αστειεύομαι.
justice	*dhikeosyni*	δικαιοσύνη

K

key	*klidhi*	κλειδί
kill	*skotono*	σκοτώνω
kind	*evyenik-os/i/o*	ευγενικ-ός/ή/ό
king	*vasilyas*	βασιλιάς
kiss (v)	*filo*	φιλώ
kiss (n)	*fili*	φιλί
knapsack	*sakkidhyo*	σακκίδιο
know (someone)	*ghnorizo*	γνωρίζω
know (something/ how to)	*xero*	ξέρω

L

lake	*limni*	λίμνη
land	*yi*	γη
landslide	*katolisthisi*	κατολίσθηση

language	*ghlossa*	γλώσσα
last (adj)	*telefte-os/a/o/*	τελευταί-ος/α/ο
late	*argh-os/i/o*	αργ-ός/ή/ό
laugh	*yelo*	γελώ
laundry	*plyndirio*	πλυντήριο
law	*nomos*	νόμος
lawyer	*dhikighoros*	δικηγόρος
lazy	*tembel-is/is/iko*	τεμπέλ-ης/α/ικο
learn	*matheno*	μαθαίνω
left	*arister-os/i/o*	αριστερ-ός/ή/ό
legal	*nomim-os/i/o*	νόμιμ-ος
less	*lighoter-os/i/o*	λιγότερ-ος/η/ο
letter	*ghramma*	γράμμα
liar	*pseftis*	ψεύτης
lice	*psirez*	ψείρες
life	*zoi*	ζωή
lift (elevator)	*asanser*	ασανσέρ
light	*fos*	φως
lighter	*anaptiras*	αναπτήρας
like (similar)	*paromi-os/a/o*	παρόμοι-ος/α/ο
like (v)	*symbatho*	συμπαθώ
I like ...	*mou aresi ...*	Μου αρέσει ...
line	*ghrammi*	γραμμή
listen	*akouo*	ακούω
little (adj)	*mikr-os/i/o*	μικρ-ός/ή/ό
live (v)	*zo*	ζω
lock (n)	*klidharya*	κλειδαριά
long	*makr-ys/ya/y*	μακρ-ύς/ιά/ύ
long ago	*edho ke polyn gero*	εδώ και πολύν καιρό
look for (v)	*psahno ya*	ψάχνω για
lose	*hano*	χάνω

lost	*hamen-os/i/o*	χαμέν-ος/η/ο
loud	*dhynat-os/i/o*	δυνατ-ός/ή/ό
love (v)	*aghapo*	αγαπώ
love (n)	*aghapi*	αγάπη
I love you.	*s'aghapo*	Σ'αγαπώ.
lucky	*tyher-os/i/o*	τυχερ-ός/ή/ό
lunch	*mesimvrino*	μεσημβρινό

M

machine	*mihani*	μηχανή
mad (crazy)	*trell-os/i/o*	τρελλ-ός/ή/ό
made of	*ftiaghmen-os/i/o apo*	φτιαγμέν-ος/η/ο από
majority	*pliopsifia*	πλειοψηφία
make	*ftiahno*	φτιάχνω
many	*poll-i/ez/a*	πολλ-οί/ές/ά
map	*hartis*	χάρτης
market	*aghora*	αγορά
marriage	*ghamos*	γάμος
marry	*pandrevome*	παντρεύομαι
massage	*masaz*	μασάζ
matches	*spirta*	σπίρτα
maybe	*isos*	ίσως
meet	*synando*	συναντώ
I'll meet you.	*tha sas synandiso*	Θα σας συναντήσω.
menu	*menou*	μενού
message	*minyma*	μήνυμα
mind (n)	*myalo*	μυαλό
minute	*lepto*	λεπτό
miss, I (feel absence of)	*mou lipi*	Μου λείπει.

VOCABULARY

mistake	*lathos*	λάθος
mix (v)	*anakatevo*	ανακατεύω
modern	*modern-os/a/o*	μοντέρν-ος/α/ο
money	*hrimata*	χρήματα
monument	*mnimio*	μνημείο
more (pl)	*periossoter-i/ez/a*	περισσότερ-οι/ες/α
morning	*proï*	πρωί
mountain	*vouno*	βουνό
mountaineering	*orivasia*	ορειβασία
movie	*kinimatoghrafiko ergho*	κινηματογραφικό έργο
museum	*mousio*	μουσείο
music	*mousiki*	μουσική

N

name	*onoma*	όνομα
national park	*ethnikos drymos*	εθνικός δρυμός
nature	*fysi*	φύση
near	*konda*	κοντά
necessary	*anange-os/a/o*	αναγκαί-ος/α/ο
neither	*oute*	ούτε
never	*pote*	ποτέ
new	*kenouri-os/a/o*	καινούρι-ος/α/ο
news	*nea*	νέα
newspaper	*efimeridha*	εφημερίδα
next	*epomen-os/i/o*	επόμεν-ος/η/-ο
night	*nyhta*	νύχτα
No.	*ohi*	Οχι.
noise	*thoryvos*	θόρυβος
noisy	*thoryvodh-is/is/ez*	θορυβώδ-ης/ης/ες
none	*tipote*	τίποτε

VOCABULARY

not any more	*pote pya*	ποτέ πια
nothing	*tipote*	τίποτε
not yet	*ohi akoma*	όχι ακόμα
now	*tora*	τώρα
nuclear energy	*pyriniki energhya*	πυρηνική ενέργεια

O

obvious	*faner-os/i/o*	φανερ-ός/ή/ό
occupation	*epangelma*	επάγγελμα
ocean	*okeanos*	ωκεανός
offend (v)	*prozvalo*	προσβάλλω
offer (v)	*prosfero*	προσφέρω
office	*ghrafio*	γραφείο
often	*syhna*	συχνά
oil	*ladhi, petrelyo*	λάδι, πετρέλαιο
old	*paly-os/a/o*	παλι-ός/ιά/ιό
on	*se*	σε
once	*mya fora*	μια φορά
one	*enas/mia/ena*	ένας/μια/ένα
only	*mono*	μόνο
open (adj)	*aniht-os/i/o*	ανοιχτ-ός/ή/ό
open (v)	*anigho*	ανοίγω
opinion	*ghnomi*	γνώμη
opportunity	*efkeria*	ευκαιρία
opposite	*apenandi*	απέναντι
or	*i*	ή
order (n)	*parangelia*	παραγγελία
ordinary	*synithizmen-os/i/o*	συνηθισμέν-ος/η/ο
organisation	*orghanosi*	οργάνωση
organise (v)	*orghanono*	οργανώνω
original	*arhik-os/i/o*	αρχικ-ός/ή/ό

other	*all-os/i/o*	άλλ-ος/η/ο
out	*exo*	έξω
outside	*ap'exo*	απ'έξω
over	*epano*	επάνω
overnight (v)	*dhianyhterevo*	διανυκτερεύω
overseas	*exoteriko*	εξωτερικό
owe (v)	*hrostao*	χρωστάω
I owe you.	*sas hrostao*	Σας χρωστάω.
You owe me.	*mou hrostate*	Μου χρωστάτε.
owner	*idhioktitis*	ιδιοκτήτης

P

package	*dhema*	δέμα
pack of cigarettes	*kouti tsighara*	κουτί τσιγάρα
packet	*paketo*	πακέτο
padlock	*louketo*	λουκέτο
painful	*odhynir-os/i/o*	οδυνηρ-ός/ή/ό
pair	*zevghari*	ζευγάρι
paper	*harti*	χαρτί
parcel	*dhema*	δέμα
park	*parko*	πάρκο
parliament	*vouli*	βουλή
part	*meros*	μέρος
participate (v)	*symeteho*	συμμετέχω
participation	*symetohi*	συμμετοχή
party	*party*	πάρτυ
party (political)	*komma*	κόμμα
passenger	*epivatis*	επιβάτης
passport	*dhiavatirio*	διαβατήριο
path	*monopati*	μονοπάτι
pay (v)	*plirono*	πληρώνω

VOCABULARY

peace	*irini*	ειρήνη
people	*kozmos*	κόσμος
perfect (adj)	*tely-os/a/o*	τέλει-ος/α/ο
permanent	*monim-os/i/o*	μόνιμ-ος/η/ο
permission	*adhya*	άδεια
permit (v)	*epitrepo*	επιτρέπω
persecution	*dhioghmos*	διωγμός
person	*atomo*	άτομο
personal	*prosopik-os/i/o*	προσωπικ-ός/ή/ό
personality	*prosopikotita*	προσωπικότητα
pharmacy	*farmakio*	φαρμακείο
photograph (n)	*fotoghrafia*	φωτογραφία
photograph (v)	*fotoghrafizo*	φωτογραφίζω
Can I take a photograph?	*boro na vghalo mya fotografia?*	Μπορώ να βγάλω μια φωτογραφία;
piece	*kommati*	κομμάτι
place	*thesi*	θέση
plane	*aeroplano*	αεροπλάνο
plant	*fyto*	φυτό
play (v)	*pezo*	παίζω
Please.	*parakalo*	Παρακαλώ.
plenty	*bolik-os/i/o*	μπόλικ-ος/η/ο
point (v)	*dhihno*	δείχνω
police	*astynomia*	αστυνομία
politics	*politika*	πολιτικά
pollution	*rypansi*	ρύπανση
pool (swimming)	*pisina*	πισίνα
poor	*ftoh-os/i/o*	φτωχ-ός/ή/ό
positive	*thetik-os/i/o*	θετικ-ός/ή/ό
postcard	*karta*	κάρτα
pottery	*keramiki*	κεραμική

VOCABULARY

poverty	*ftohya*	φτώχεια
power	*dhynami*	δύναμη
practical	*praktik-os/i/o*	πρακτικ-ός/ή/ό
prayer	*efhi*	ευχή
prefer	*protimo*	προτιμώ
pregnant	*engyos*	έγκυος
present (time)	*paron*	παρόν
present (gift)	*dhoro*	δώρο
president	*proedhros*	πρόεδρος
pretty	*omorf-os/i/o*	όμορφ-ος/η/ο
prevent	*embodhizo*	εμποδίζω
price	*timi*	τιμή
priest	*pappas*	παππάς
prime minister	*prothypourghos*	πρωθυπουργός
prison	*fylaki*	φυλακή
prisoner (m & f)	*fylakizmen-os/i*	φυλακισμέν-ος/η
private	*idhiotik-os/i/o*	ιδιωτικ-ός/ή/ό
probably	*mallon*	μάλλον
problem	*provlima*	πρόβλημα
procession	*poria*	πορεία
produce (v)	*paragho*	παράγω
professional	*epangelmatik-os/i/o*	επαγγελματικ-ός/ή/ό
profit	*kerdhos*	κέρδος
promise (n)	*yposhesi*	υπόσχεση
promise (v)	*yposhome*	υπόσχομαι
prostitute	*porni*	πόρνη
protect	*prostatevo*	προστατεύω
protest (n)	*dhiamartyrome*	διαμαρτύρομαι
public	*dhimosi-os/a/o*	δημόσι-ος/α/ο
pull	*travo*	τραβώ
push	*sprohno*	σπρώχνω

Q

quality	*piyotita*	ποιότητα
question (n)	*erotisi*	ερώτηση
quick	*ghrighor-os/i/o*	γρήγορ-ος/η/ο
quiet	*isih-os/i/o*	ήσυχ-ος/η/ο

R

race (contest)	*aghonas*	αγώνας
racist	*ratsistis*	ρατσιστής
radio	*radhiofono*	ραδιόφωνο
railway	*sidhirodhromos*	σιδηρόδρομος
rain	*vrohi*	βροχή
raining, It's	*vrehi*	βρέχει.
rape (n)	*viazmos*	βιασμός
rape (v)	*viazo*	βιάζω
rare	*spani-os/a/o*	σπάνι-ος/α/ο
raw	*om-ós/í/ó*	ωμ-ός/ή/ό
ready	*etim-os/i/o*	έτοιμ-ος/η/ο
reason	*etia*	αιτία
receipt	*apodhixi*	απόδειξη
recently	*prosfata*	πρόσφατα
recommend	*synisto*	συνιστώ
refugee	*prosfyghas*	πρόσφυγας
refund	*epistrofi hrimaton*	επιστροφή χρημάτων
refuse	*arnoume*	αρνούμαι
region	*periohi*	περιοχή
regulation	*kanonizmos*	κανονισμός
relationship	*syngenia*	συγγένεια
relax	*xekourazome*	ξεκουράζομαι

VOCABULARY

VOCABULARY

religion	*thriskia*	θρησκεία
remember	*thymame*	θυμάμαι
remote	*apomer-os/i/o*	απόμερ-ος/η/ο
rent (n)	*enikio*	ενοίκιο
rent (v)	*nikyazo*	νοικιάζω
representative	*andiprosopos*	αντιπρόσωπος
republic	*dhimokratia*	δημοκρατία
reservation	*kratisi*	κράτηση
reserve (v)	*klino*	κλείνω
respect (n)	*sevazmos*	σεβασμός
responsibility	*efthyni*	ευθύνη
rest (relaxation) (n)	*xekourasi*	ξεκούραση
restaurant	*estiatorio*	εστιατόριο
return (v)	*epistrefo*	επιστρέφω
revolution	*epanastasi*	επανάσταση
rich	*plousi-os/a/o*	πλούσι-ος/α/ο
right (opposite of left)	*dhexi-os/a/o*	δεξι-ός/ά/ό
right, I'm	*eho dhikio*	έχω δίκιο
risk	*kindhynos*	κίνδυνος
road	*dhromos*	δρόμος
robber	*kleftis*	κλέφτης
robbery	*klopi*	κλοπή
roof	*steghi*	στέγη
room	*dhomatio*	δωμάτιο
rope	*shini*	σχοινί
round	*strongyl-os/i/o*	στρόγγυλ-ος/η/ο
rubbish	*skoupidhya*	σκουπίδια
ruins	*arhea*	αρχαία
rule	*kanonas*	κανόνας

S

sad	*stenahori-men-os/i/o*	στεναχωρη-μένο-ος/η/ο
safe (n)	*hrimatokivotio*	χρηματοκιββώτιο
safe (adj)	*asfal-is/is/ez*	ασφαλ-ής/ής/ές
safety	*asfalya*	ασφάλεια
salty	*almyr-os/i/o*	αλμυρ-ός/ή/ό
same	*idhi-os/a/o*	ίδι-ος/α/ο
scenery	*thea*	θέα
seasickness	*naftia*	ναυτία
secret	*mystiko*	μυστικό
selfish	*idhiotel-is/is/ez*	ιδιοτελ-ής/ής/ές
sell	*poulao*	πουλάω
send	*stelno*	στέλνω
serious	*sovar-os/i/o*	σοβαρ-ός/ή/ό
several	*kambos-i/ez/a*	κάμποσ-οι/ες/α
shade (n)	*iskios*	ίσκιος
share (v)	*mirazo*	μοιράζω
share (n)	*meridhio*	μερίδιο
short (time)	*ligh-os/i/o*	λίγ-ος/η/ο
short (height)	*kond-os/i/o*	κοντ-ός/ή/ό
shortage	*ellipsi*	έλλειψη
shout (v)	*fonazo*	φωνάζω
show (v)	*dhihno*	δείχνω
Show me.	*dhixte mou*	Δείξτε μου.
shut (adj)	*klist-os/i/o*	κλειστ-ός/ή/ό
shut (v)	*klino*	κλείνω
shy	*dropal-os/i/o*	ντροπαλ-ός/ή/ό
sick	*arrosto-os/i/o*	άρρωστ-ος/η/ο
sickness	*arrostia*	αρρώστεια
sign	*sima*	σήμα

similar	*paromi-os/a/o*	παρόμοι-ος/α/ο
since	*apo*	από
single (unmarried)	*anypandr-os/i/o*	ανύπαντρ-ος/η/ο
sit	*kathome*	κάθομαι
situation	*katastasi*	κατάσταση
size	*meghethos*	μέγεθος
sleep (v)	*kimame*	κοιμάμαι
sleep (n)	*ypnos*	ύπνος
sleepy (to be)	*nystazo*	νυστάζω
slow	*argh-os/i/o*	αργ-ός/ή/ό
slowly	*argha*	αργά
small	*mikr-os/i/o*	μικρ-ός/ή/ό
smell (n)	*myrodhya*	μυρωδιά
socialism	*sosializmos*	σοσιαλισμός
solid	*yer-os/i/o*	γερ-ός/ή/ό
some	*merik-i/ez/a*	μερικ-οί/ές/ά
somebody	*kapyos, kapya*	κάποιος (m)
		κάποια (f)
something	*kati*	κάτι
sometimes	*kamya fora*	καμμιά φορά
song	*traghoudi*	τραγούδι
soon	*syndoma*	σύντομα
sorry, I'm	*lypame*	λυπάμαι
souvenir	*enthymio*	ενθύμιο
special	*idhik-os/i/o*	ειδικ-ός/ή/ό
sport	*athlima*	άθλημα
standard (adj)	*kanonik-os/i/o*	κανονικ-ός/ή/ό
stay (n)	*paramoni*	παραμονή
stay (v)	*mino*	μείνω
steal	*klevo*	κλέβω
stop (v)	*stamatao*	σταματάω
story (tale)	*paramythi*	παραμύθι

straight	*efth-ys/ia/y*	ευθ-ύς/εία/ύ
strange	*paraxen-os/i/o*	παράξεν-ος/η/ο
stranger	*xenos*	ξένος
street	*odhos*	οδός
strong	*dhynat-os/i/o*	δυνατ-ός/ή/ό
stupid	*haz-os/i/o*	χαζ-ός/ή/ό
suddenly	*xafnika*	ξαφνικά
sunglasses	*yalya iliou*	γυαλιά ηλίου
sure	*sighour-os/i/o*	σίγουρ-ος/η/ο
surprise	*ekplixi*	έκπληξη
I'm surprised.	*ekplisome*	Εκπλήσσομαι.
sweet	*ghlyk-ys/ia/y*	γλυκ-ύς/ιά/ύ
swim (v)	*kolimbo*	κολυμπώ

T

take	*perno*	παίρνω
talk (v)	*milao*	μιλάω
tall	*psil-os/i/o*	ψηλ-ός/ή/ό
tasty	*nostim-os/i/o*	νόστιμ-ος/η/ο
tax	*foros*	φόρος
telephone (n)	*tilefono*	τηλέφωνο
telephone (v)	*tilefono*	τηλεφωνώ
telephone book	*tilefonikos kataloghos*	τηλεφωνικός κατάλογος
temperature (weather)	*thermokrasia*	θερμοκρασία
temperature (fever)	*pyretos*	πυρετός
tent	*skini*	σκηνή
thank	*efharisto*	ευχαριστώ
Thank you.	*sas efharisto*	Σας ευχαριστώ.
there	*eki*	εκεί

VOCABULARY

thick	hondr-os/i/o	χοντρ-ός/ή/ό
thief	kleftis	κλέφτης
thin	lept-os/i/o	λεπτ-ός/ή/ό
think	nomizo	νομίζω
thirsty (to be)	dhipsao	δειψάω
ticket	isitirio	εισιτήριο
time	ora	ώρα
What time is it?	ti ora ine?	Τι ώρα είναι;
tip (gratuity)	filodhorima, 'pour boire'	φιλοδόρημα, πουρμπουάρ
tired, I'm	kourastika	κουράστηκα
together	mazi	μαζί
toilet	toualetta	τουαλέττα
toilet paper	harti iyias	χαρτί υγείας
tonight	apopse	απόψε
too	episis	επίσης
toothbrush	odhondovourtsa	οδοντόβουρτσα
toothpaste	odhontokrema	οδοντόκρεμα
torch (flashlight)	fakos	φακός
touch (v)	angizo	αγγίζω
tour	ekdromi	εκδρομή
tourist	touristas	τουρίστας
toward	pros	προς
town	komopoli	κωμόπολη
track	monopati	μονοπάτι
transit (in)	tranzito	τράνζιτο
translate	metafrazo	μεταφράζω
trekking	odhiporia	οδοιπορία
trip	taxidhi	ταξίδι
true	alithin-os/i/o	αληθιν-ός/ή/ό
trust	embistosyni	εμπιστοσύνη
try	dhokimazo	δοκιμάζω

VOCABULARY

U

uncomfortable	*avoul-os/i/o*	άβουλ-ος/η/ο
under	*kato apo*	κάτω από
understand	*katalaveno*	καταλαβαίνω
I don't understand.	*dhen katalaveno*	Δεν καταλαβαίνω.
unemployed	*anergh-os/i/o*	άνεργ-ος/η/ο
university	*panepistimio*	πανεπιστήμιο
unsafe	*anasfal-is/is/es*	ανασφαλ-ής/ής/ές
until	*mehri*	μέχρι
up	*pano*	πάνω
upstairs	*epano*	επάνω
useful	*hrisim-os/i/o*	χρήσιμ-ος/η/ο

V

vacation	*dhiakopez*	διακοπές
vaccination	*emvoliazmos*	εμβολιασμός
valuable	*polytim-os/i/o*	πολύτιμ-ος/η/ο
value (price)	*axia*	αξία
very	*poly*	πολύ
view (n)	*thea*	θέα
village	*horio*	χωριό
visit (v)	*episkeftome*	επισκέφτομαι
vomit (v)	*kano emeto*	κάνω εμετό
vote (v)	*psifizo*	ψηφίζω

W

wait	*perimeno*	περιμένω
walk	*perpato*	περπατώ
want	*thelo*	θέλω
I want ...	*(egho) thelo ...*	(Εγώ) θέλω ...

VOCABULARY

Do you want ...?	*thelete ...?*	Θέλετε ... ;
war	*polemos*	πόλεμος
warm	*zest-os/i/ó*	ζεστ-ός/ή/ό
wash (yourself)	*plenome*	πλένομαι
wash (clothes, etc)	*pleno*	πλένω
watch (v)	*kitazo*	κοιτάζω
watch (timepiece)	*roloyi*	ρολόι
water	*nero*	νερό
way	*dhromos*	δρόμος
Which way?	*apo pou?*	Από πού;
wealthy	*plousi-os/a/o*	πλούσι-ος/α/ο
weather	*keros*	καιρός
Welcome!	*kalosorisate!*	Καλωσορίσατε!
well (n)	*sterna*	στέρνα
wet	*vreghmen-os/i/o*	βρεγμέν-ος/η/ο
what	*ti*	τι
What time is it?	*ti ora ine?*	Τι ώρα είναι;
What did you say?	*signomi, ti ipate?*	Συγγνώμη, τι είπατε;
when	*pote*	Πότε
When is the next boat to ...?	*pote fevyi to epomeno karavi ya tin ...?*	Πότε φεύγει το επόμενο καράβι για την ...;
where	*pou*	πού
Where is ...?	*pou ine ...?*	Πού είναι ...;
who	*pios*	ποιος
Who do I ask?	*pyon tha ritiso?*	Ποιον θα ρωτήσω;
win	*kerdhizo*	κερδίζω
wise	*sof-os/i/ó*	σοφ-ός/ή/ό
with	*me*	με
within	*mesa*	μέσα
without	*horis*	χωρίς

work (v)	*dhoulevo*	δουλεύω
work (n)	*dhoulya*	δουλειά
world	*kozmos*	κόσμος
worse	*hiroter-os/i/o*	χειρότερ-ος/η/ο
write	*ghrafo*	γράφω
wrong	*lanthazmen-os/i/o*	λανθασμέν-ος/η/ο

Y

year	*etos*	έτος
... years ago	*edho kai ... hronia*	εδώ και ... χρόνια
Yes.	*ne*	Ναι.
yesterday	*hthes*	χθες
young	*ne-os/a/o*	νέ-ος/α/ο

Z

| zone | *zoni* | ζώνη |
| zoo | *zo-ologhikos kipos* | ζωολογικός κήπος |

VOCABULARY

Emergencies

We hope that your visit to Greece or Cyprus will not be marred by any nasty situations, but it's better to be prepared than sorry. It might be a good idea if you have a look at this section before you need it. Learn the basic phrases and practise them with the help of a Greek friend. Then go and enjoy yourself!

Help!	*voithya!*	Βοήθεια!
Watch out!	*prosohi!*	Προσοχή!
Go away!	*fighe!*	Φύγε!
Get lost!	*hasou!*	Χάσου!
Stop it!	*stamata!*	Σταμάτα!
Police!	*astinomia!*	Αστυνομία!
Thief!	*klefti!*	Κλέφτη!

Call a doctor!
  fonaxte ena yatro!　　　Φωνάξτε ένα ιατρό.
There's been an accident.
  eyine atihima　　　Εγινε ατύχημα.
Call an ambulance.
  tilefoniste ya asthenoforo　　　Τηλεφωνήστε για
　　　ασθενοφόρο.

I am ill.
  ime arostos　　　Είμαι άρρωστος.
I am lost.
  eho hathi　　　Εχω χαθεί.
I've been raped.
  me viase kapyos　　　Με βίασε κάποιος.
I've been robbed.
  meklepse kapyos　　　Μ'έκλεψε κάποιος.

I've lost …

my bag	*tin dzanda mou*	την τσάντα μου
my money	*ta lefta mou*	τα λεφτά μου
my passport	*to dhiavatirio mou*	το διαβατήριό μου
my travellers' cheques	*tis taxidhiotikez mou epitayez*	τις ταξιδιωτικές μου επιταγές

eho hasi …   Εχω χάσει …

Could I use the telephone?
*boro na hrisimopiiso
to tilefono?*

Μπορώ να χρησιμοποιήσω
το τηλέφωνο;

I have medical insurance.
eho yatriki asfalya

Εχω ιατρική ασφάλεια.

Index

Language Survival Kits

Complete your travel experience with a Lonely Planet phrasebook. Developed for the independent traveller, the phrasebooks enable you to communicate confidently in any practical situation – and get to know the local people and their culture.

Skipping lengthy details on where to get your drycleaning ironed, information in the phrasebooks covers bargaining, customs and protocol, how to address people and introduce yourself, explanations of local ways of telling the time, dealing with bureaucracy and bargaining, plus plenty of ways to share your interests and learn from locals.

Australian
Introduction to Australian English, Aboriginal and Torres Strait languages.
Arabic (Egyptian)
Arabic (Moroccan)
Brazilian
Burmese
Cantonese
Central Europe
Covers Czech, French, German, Hungarian, Italian and Slovak.
Eastern Europe
Covers Bulgarian, Czech, Hungarian, Polish, Romanian and Slovak.
Fijian
Greek
Hindi/Urdu
Indonesian
Japanese
Korean
Mandarin
Mediterranean Europe
Covers Albanian, Greek, Italian, Macedonian, Maltese, Serbian & Croatian and Slovene.

Nepali
Pidgin
Pilipino
Quechua
Russian
Scandinavian Europe
Covers Danish, Finnish, Icelandic, Norwegian and Swedish.
Spanish (Latin American)
Sri Lanka
Swahili
Thai
Thai Hill Tribes
Tibet
Turkish
US
Introduction to US English, Vernacular Talk, Native American languages and Hawaiian.
Vietnamese
Western Europe
Useful words and phrases in Basque, Catalan, Dutch, French, German, Irish, Portugese and Spanish (Castilian).

Lonely Planet Audio Packs

The best way to learn a language is to hear it spoken in context. Set within a dramatic narrative, with local music and local speakers, is a wide range of words and phrases for the independent traveller – to help you talk to people you meet, make your way around more easily, and enjoy your stay.

Each pack includes a phrasebook and CD or cassette, and comes in an attractive, useful cloth bag. These bags are made by local community groups, using traditional methods.

Forthcoming Language Survival Kits
Baltic States (Estonian, Latvian and Lithuanian), Lao, Mongolian, Bengali, Sinhalese, Hebrew, Ukrainian

Forthcoming Audio Packs
Indonesian, Japanese, Thai, Vietnamese, Mandarin, Cantonese

LONELY PLANET PUBLICATIONS
Australia: PO Box 617, Hawthorn, Victoria 3122
USA: 155 Filbert Street, Suite 251, Oakland CA 94607
UK: 10 Barley Mow Passage, Chiswick, London W4 4PH
France: 71 bis, rue du Cardinal Lemoine – 75005 Paris